MATERIALIEN
FÜR DIE SEKUNDARSTUFE II

DIESTERWEGS
NEUSPRACHLICHE
ARBEITSMITTEL

How to deal with texts

Teacher's Manual

Reinhard Kemnitz
Norbert Köhn
Friederike Podziemski
John Podziemski

DIESTERWEG

Druck A [9] / Jahr 2014
Alle Drucke der Serie A sind im Unterricht parallel verwendbar.

Umschlaggestaltung: Werbeatelier Richter, Seeheim-Jugenheim
Satz: Fotosatz Otto Gutfreund, Darmstadt
Druck und Bindung: westermann druck GmbH, Braunschweig

ISBN 978-3-425-**00432**-7

Contents

* excerpt from a complete work of the same title

Chapter III: Point of View

Chapter IV: Plot and Characters

Chapter V: Stylistic Devices

Introduction

The principal ideas that lie behind this text analysis project have already been referred to in the introduction to the student's book on *How to deal with texts*. Therefore, we felt it unnecessary to repeat these ideas in this brief introduction to the teacher's manual. Instead, a few remarks on the layout of this manual, on the content format of the entries, and on the suggested usage of the student's book would seem more appropriate here.

In the main the questions set in the student's book have been answered with a degree of comprehensiveness, although the answers are by no means definitive, nor are the quotes from the individual texts as back-up evidence exhaustive. And while the answers are attempts at covering the ground under investigation the texts can still be studied in even greater depth. The only omissions to be made in this manual are any responses to the creative writing tasks and references to the suggestions for discussions. The creative writing exercise is an integral part of each topic at hand, but also leaves ample scope for personal inventiveness and imagination; we decided therefore that it was better not to interfere. The suggestions for discussions should be based chiefly on points taken from the individual texts, and as a certain amount of repetition would have been unavoidable we decided not to include any comments on this section. Moreover, in this systematic approach to text analysis, while the tasks just mentioned fit in neatly to the approach, they can be left out at will. This should not be the case with the rest of the questions.

We suggest two ways of approaching the student's book in order to get the greatest benefit from it. (A third "method", simply studying individual texts more or less arbitrarily is of course also possible.) Let us take a look at these two approaches in a little more detail. Both the five chapters in the book and the individual texts in each chapter can be dealt with chronologically. Thus the student should be well-equipped to look at texts more rewardingly. Alternatively, particular chapters could be selected from time to time as and when the situation arises (each chapter is also organised in a systematic fashion); for example, the problem of plot and character might arise when studying a full-length novel; or when discussing poetry one might wish to spend some more time looking at stylistic devices. As you can see, although the project is firmly based on a systematic approach to text analysis, there is still a large degree of flexibility possible.

In conclusion, we hope that in using this text analysis book the study of texts, whether fictional or non-fictional, will become less arduous and in due course more fun because of the wide choice of different text forms and because of the systematic approach that links all manner of texts together. Finally, the authors would welcome any remarks and criticisms, which could then be integrated into the book and ultimately be of benefit to the student.

Note: The terminology used in the theoretical sections of the student's book and in this manual is not rooted in one particular school of thought but has been chosen instead on the principles of lucidity and practicability. This approach seemed all the more justified as in many cases there are no uniform and binding concepts, especially the terminology connected with point of view.

Chapter I

Text-Categories and Forms

1. Genesis

1. This story is about man's pride and arrogance (hubris), which makes him unwilling to accept anyone above him, even including God. In an incorrigible attempt to outdo God's miracles with the help of scientific inventions man finally destroys the earth and himself. God, of course, lives on, and He "can raise the dead", i. e. start creation anew.

2. This text is a fictional text as can easily be seen by the number of invented elements. There is, firstly, God's appearance in the story as a "stranger" working Biblical miracles; secondly, the scientific inventions employed in the story are within the range of feasibility, but not yet all reality; thirdly, the end of the story presents the complete destruction of the earth, an event which is obviously not factual. A further source of evidence that prompts a classification of this story as fictional is the lack of precise information. The time and scene of action are not specified nor is the name of the Prime Minister given. The social and political conditions are not described either, nor is there even a hint at what God will do after the destruction of the world.

3. This text belongs to the group of short narrative fiction. The limited number of characters, the concentration solely on this 'miracle challenge' between God and man, the immediacy of the story's beginning, and the open, surprise ending are all criteria that can be found in a short story. In this case there are also parallels to the *parable*, whose purpose it is to teach people by means of an example. The aim of this text can be interpreted as a warning to man not to believe in his own perfection nor to glorify science and technology as the modern equivalents of God. In this context the absence of precise factual information acquires greater significance: the application of the message of this story is meant to put the scope of the individual, nations, or society into perspective. The text aims at universal validity through the presentation of a typical case open to generalisation.

2. The Rabbits Who Caused All The Trouble

1. This text is about the abuse of power and the discrimination against and oppression of a defenceless minority. Using a number of quite

absurd accusations and prejudices the powerful wolves make a family of rabbits their scapegoats and justify the constant threatening and final destruction of the rabbits.

2. This text can be classified as a fictional text as it contains quite a number of invented elements. Of course there are wolves and rabbits in the real world but this text describes an artifically constructed imaginary world in which animals are endowed with human characteristics and abilities (language, the ability of reasoning, prejudices, abuse of power, discrimination). Another piece of evidence to prove the fictional nature of the text is its lack of details and precise information. There is no information at all given on the scene of action, and the time of action is only very vaguely hinted at ("Within the memory of the youngest child..."). The "other animals" are not specified, except for the fact that they "lived at a great distance".

As this text does not strive after objectivity its evaluative quality prevails. Though there is very little explicit evaluation to be found in the text, quite a number of evaluations are presented implicitly as can be seen by the use of accusations, which are clearly recognizable as dangerous prejudices, or in the use of subtle irony: the way the wolves are living is claimed to be "the only way to live"; there is also evaluation in the ironical remarks that "the wolves descended on the rabbits, for their own good..." or that eaten rabbits are "a purely internal matter".

3. This text is a fable. The principle characteristic of a fable is that it is a short story that exemplifies a moral thesis or a principle of human behaviour. Most common is the beast fable, in which animals are presented acting and talking like human beings. Usually in its conclusion either the narrator or one of the characters states a moral. All these criteria are to be found in the text under discussion. The above mentioned lack of precise information on the time and scene of the action is a further characteristic feature of a fable. Detailed information is irrelevant for the fable's intention as it concentrates exclusively on one typical, though significant, aspect of life. Thus it is not able to present anything other than a limited view of the world. Detailed information would therefore particularize an event and hinder its generalization. The concentration on one significant aspect of life serves the fable's purpose of exemplification, generalization, and universal validity.

The moral takes the form of an instruction. Its message is rather vague and can be interpreted as a piece of advice to avoid conformity and to resist unjust authority.

3. The Zoo Story

1. One man addresses another in a park and almost forces him into a somewhat confused conversation about the former's visit to the zoo, and about its position in relation to the park.

2. The fictional nature of this text is identifiable on the basis of two direct references, firstly, the fact that the people presented are referred to initially as 'characters' and, secondly, that the word "stage" is explicitly mentioned. On a closer look the fictional quality of the text, in contrast to a factual description, can also be underlined by other criteria. Although the reader is provided with a lot of information enabling him to gain a precise idea of the characters involved and the time and scene of the action, these pieces of information are so vague that no one-to-one correspondence with the real world is possible. Peter and Jerry would appear to be two Americans who live in New York and meet in Central Park one Sunday afternoon in summer in the present. The characterisations of Peter and Jerry could apply to many people; the 'present' time corresponds to when the text was written and changes according to when the text is read, thus applying always. Only the references to Central Park and to some street names are factually identifiable, but it does not become obvious why they are of any contextual relevance. Another pointer to the fictional quality of the text lies in the way Jerry and Peter are characterised, which is not meant merely to convey an objective impression of them but clearly contains elements of evaluation, especially in the case of Jerry. Thus, despite the fact that none of the elements mentioned in the text are factually impossible or even improbable, the fictional quality does prevail.

3. This text is the beginning of a play. The typographical layout already reveals some basic characteristics of this text form. There are four recognizable types of print: capital letters to indicate who is spoken about (see stage directions) or who speaks; another layout to characterise the actors; yet another to describe the time and the scene of the action, and the behaviour of the actors; and the last to reproduce the dialogue between the actors. Of these four only the last is directly presented on the stage; everything else is, more or less completely, incorporated in the stage props, the personalities of the actors, their gestures and dramatic flair. It becomes clear from the classification of this text as a play that no direct mirror image of real life is intended, but that characters and circumstances are chosen so as to guarantee a broader interpretable reflexion of life. What would have to be judged as a severe flaw in a

factual, descriptive text turns out not only to be intended, but also necessary, for a fictional text that seeks to deal with more general truths.

4. The Hangman at Home

1. The poem presents the speaker's reflections on a hangman's dealings with his circumstances in life, concentrating on the conflicting patterns of work versus family life. The hangman's demeanour in a number of situations at home, the family's responses, and his formation of a philosophy of life are investigated in connection with his destructive practice at work.

2. The text concentrates on the time a hangman spends with his family, describing situations very close to everyday life. Nevertheless, the fictional quality of this text clearly prevails in that the speaker makes no attempt at an exact reconstruction of the situations, but rather reflects generally on the mutual perception and dealings of the family as well as on the way they talk and on what they say. Secondly, this poem lacks a comprehensible time sequence and a precise location. Thirdly, it abounds in rhetorical questions intended to influence the reader. The choice of situations is clearly selective, including *suggestive* elements, e.g. the focus on the hangman's hands at the meal (ll. 11/12), the game with his children using a rope (ll. 13–16). Finally, the explicit evaluation in the last line of the poem ("I guess") also contributes to the fictional quality of this text.

3. The outer presentation of this text makes it clearly identifiable as a poem, although it lacks a conventionalised structure, rhyme scheme, or a regular metre. There is, however, extensive use of stylistic devices such as anaphora (e.g. "when", ll. 2/3; "and", ll. 10/11) and run-on lines, giving this poem a narrative style. Thus the language remains within the bounds of accepted usage, being quite commonplace. Nevertheless, the language is also highly allusive (see the interpretative impact of "hands" in line 12 and "rope" in lines 15f.). It is also worth noting the accumulation of rhetorical questions and the recurrent use of the subjunctive.

This poem recreates a topic of general significance, stimulating a controversial discussion. This is partly due to the subjective and provocative presentation of the theme. This lack of neutrality helps to create an awareness regarding capital punishment and the death sentence, about the people involved in and suffering from this system, about the ethical obligations of the state concerning vital human rights, and about the fundamental values of a society.

5. Scotland

1. This text shows two aspects of Scotland. There is first the commercial aspect, which is illustrated by the effects the change of energy resources – from whale-oil to gas and oil – have had on Aberdeen and its inhabitants. And then there is the other, "wild" Scotland, which does not seem to have changed since 1745.

2. This text contains a lot of factual information about Scotland which could easily be checked against the reality or by means of reference books (e.g. to see whether you can "see men wearing a Stetson hat in any part of Aberdeen" or whether Aberdeen is really "the third biggest fishing port in Britain" or whether "Marshal Wade was sent to build roads in the Highlands"). The aim of these statements is certainly to inform the reader of important facts in the past and present history of Scotland. There is, however, another group of words and phrases which is not concerned with objective description but with subjective impressions and evaluation (e.g. "*evocative* names", "oil-drilling *fraternity*"; "we tend to be very sceptical"; "A fine code of politeness flowers from touching your hat..."). The author openly admits his subjective involvement by talking of his own experience ("When I was a boy") and that of his people of which he considers himself a typical representative ("we have a long history in Scotland"). This mixture of objective description and subjective evaluation classifies this text as 'factional'.

3. This text belongs to the group of travel reports which seek to inform the reader on places and sights, landscape and people, of a country, region, or city. But they aim at more than just the provision of information contained in much greater detail and accuracy in reference books. They aim to present a vivid and interesting view, insider information, sights, events and phenomena no one has even seen or experienced before with the intention of whetting the reader's appetite and inspiring him to attempt a similar journey himself. This undeniable element of manipulative practice leads to the inclusion of humorous episodes, thrilling adventures, encounters, accidents, comparisons with travellers in the past and, of course, the indispensible, 'infallible', ironic, cynical or benevolent judgment of the author. In this text it is obviously benevolence and national pride that dominate, together with subjective evaluation mixed with a sadness tinged with fear that "wild" Scotland could be "civilized" by progress.

6. The Science to save us from Science

1. This text presents the question as to whether the rapid development of scientific discovery and invention during the past 350 years now poses a threat to the existence of mankind. A preliminary to the final answer is whether science will advance as rapidly in the future as it has done in the past. Russell believes that because of the support through universities and governments, the improvement in teaching methods, the increasing specialization, and its attraction for great minds scientific progress will not slow down.

2. This text deals with a subject (science) that normally demands logic in composition, objectivity of presentation and plainness of style and that is usually associated with a high frequency of technical terms, thus making it difficult for a lay reader to understand. This text is different. There are references to scientific inventions, but only a few, and the references are to the more generally known ones; philosophers and artists are more frequently quoted than scientists; and, most astonishingly, the style of the text is not at all plain and easily digestible. Moreover, the author does not refrain from occasionally giving his personal opinion ("I suppose"; "I do not think", "alas"). This mixture of objective discourse and individually tinted presentation marks this as a 'factional' text.

3. This text takes the form of an essay. Characteristic features of the essay are that subjects from every sector of life are discussed in a discriminating, yet aesthetically pleasing form. Subjectivity of judgment is an integral part of the essay, as it is the author's view on a subject and his proposed solution to problems that the essay is really about. The dividing line between information and manipulation is intentionally abolished. The author wants to influence the reader with his opinion, mostly in order to make him familiar with a problem and provide him with subjectively appropriate answers. Very often an essay reveals more about the *Zeitgeist* of the period than about the subject itself.

7. I have a Dream

1. This text presents the vision that the fundamental statement of the Declaration of Independence of the United States of America, "all men are created equal", will come true one day and that the present situation of racial injustice and discrimination will be overcome and substituted by freedom, equality, and brotherhood.

2. There are a lot of factual references and pieces of information based

on present reality mentioned in this text which could be checked and proven to belong to the real world, e.g. the states and mountain ranges of the U.S.A. mentioned; the present situation of racial injustice and oppression of black people, especially in the southern states of the U.S.A.; the possibility of American states to refuse to recognize a Federal law ("interposition and nullification"); and last but not least the highly important passage of the Declaration of Independence.

On the other hand the speaker sets forth his own dream of an American nation granting equal rights to everybody irrespective of colour or religion. Though these visions may possibly and hopefully be reality one day, they are not reality yet but only extremely subjective prophesies ("With this faith we will be able to transform the jangling discords... into a beautiful symphony of brotherhood."). Therefore the text contains a large number of highly emotional and evaluative expressions and comments, such as "sweltering with the heat of oppression", "vicious racists", "his lips dripping with words of interposition and nullification". This combination of objective references to the United States of America and subjective evaluation and visions makes this text a 'factional' one.

3. This text belongs to the group of political speeches. Characteristic elements of a political speech are that it seeks to influence, manipulate, convince or motivate its audience. It is always based on past or present reality and contains subjective elements of evaluation and judgment which are essential parts of a political speech. All these criteria are to be found in this text. It seeks to motivate its audience to keep struggling for a better society for their children to live in. The speaker wants to convince people by his faith and prophesies that fighting and suffering for the equal rights of black Americans is worth while and that this aim is within the range of probable future realization. The often almost biblical language shows that this particular speech is closely related to a sermon though its politically explosive nature and imperious political character clearly mark it as a political speech.

8. Beatable and Unbeatable

1. This text deals with the legitimacy of corporal punishment in some state schools in Great Britain, especially after the European Court of Human Rights decided against it. The solution arrived at, namely, to allow parents to exempt their children from corporal punishment implies the unequal treatment of children in the same school. The other possible

solutions – a general ban; a ban in some schools so that parents could have the option of sending their children to a school of their choice; disregard for the European legislation on this matter – all seemed impracticable in terms of education, cost, and reputation.

2. This text concentrates on events which are taken from real life and could theoretically be proved with ease by consulting the judges or government spokesmen responsible, or even Sir Keith Joseph, who is mentioned in the text. The subject is, moreover, so topical and of vital concern to many parents that the publication of inaccurate statements in a newspaper would be spotted and could lead to protest. But although this text does not contain invented or violently distorted elements, the factual information remains fragmentary and lacking in detail. Instead, the author openly voices his own opinion on the subject, thus clearly seeking to influence the reader (e.g. "It is easy to appreciate the Government's dilemma."). In this mixture of basic objective information and subjective judgment the text is seen to be 'factional'.

3. This text is a newspaper leader or editorial, in which the editor of a newspaper is given the opportunity of commenting on an important piece of news which is factually presented in some other part of the same edition of the paper. Only enough factual information is provided to enable the reader to envisage the problem. The real purpose of the article is to provoke critical discussion of the item under consideration, explicitly aiming at manipulating public opinion. As the topic of a commentary is normally politically tinged the conclusions and judgment presented in it mirror the political stance of the newspaper. The same kind of relation can be found between the stylistic level of composition and the social target group aimed at by the newspaper.

9. Citroën

1. This text points out the advantages of a car called the Citroën 2 CV such as wheels, windows, braking system (in other words, the basics) and what is included in the price of £ 2499.

2. This text is about a car which most people will have probably seen at some time or other on the roads. Basically, the reader does not learn anything new or excitingly revolutionary about the properties of this car; after all, "round wheel", "transparent windows", and a "braking system" worked by a pedal are the characteristic and invariably essential features of all cars today. The basic features are manipulated linguistically (inverted) to appear technologically advanced. Thus straightforward

information is obviously not the central concern of this text; the humorous presentation underlines this fact. The author's main interest lies in passing on his evaluation of the car, which is unreservedly positive. The text, therefore, is 'factional'.

3. This text is an advertisement whose aim it is to persuade the reader to buy a certain product (very often this is done using a combination of text and picture). The formula AIDA describes the desired response the advertisement seeks to evoke: *attention*, *interest*, *desire*, *action*. *Attention* is aroused by the juxtaposition of the heading that "there's nothing to go wrong" with the picture of the car referred to. The 2 CV is normally associated with a certain primitiveness rather than with automobile sophistication. *Interest* is stimulated by the enumeration of qualities which are by no means special in themselves but which are cited as if they were the unique achievement of this car. By suggesting that the technical equipment of larger models (e.g. central locking system) is superfluous luxury made necessary by their awkward size or by the laziness of their owners (cf. automatic sunshine roof) this advertisement indirectly portrays the potential owner of the 2 CV – young, active, individualistic, sensible, in favour of low fuel consumption, opposed to affluence and superfluity – and aims at stimulating the *desire* in the reader to purchase this product and thus identify with this type of person. The *action* is, of course, the purchase of the product, for one's own pleasure and the industry's profit.

10. Kicking the Hospital Habit

1. Brian Inglis discusses the demand for increased financial support for the NHS as put forward in the *New Statesman*. He rejects this proposal and argues in favour of a useful limitation of the escalation of costs in the NHS. He also suggests a massive change in the distribution of finances available to the NHS as well as a de-monopolisation of the medical profession.

2. This text is devoted to a problem of great topicality for the public. The text deals with factual elements such as the distribution of NHS funds, the payment of doctors, and orthodox medicine. The principal aim of this text, however, is not to inform objectively but to deliver a personal opinion on these aspects of the National Health Service. Brian Inglis expresses his dissatisfaction with current practices within the NHS and demands concrete changes. Among the changes proposed are the setting-up and the application of preventive medicine, thus minimising

treatment in hospitals and reducing the number of in-patients as well as deviating from orthodox medicine and increasingly using alternative forms of medical treatment. This juxtaposition of factual elements and an explicitly personal conviction clearly renders this text as 'factional'.

3. This text conveys the typical appearance of a letter to the editor of a newspaper in that it
- gives the writer's name and address
- shows clear references (date and source of publication) to the article complained about
- addresses the writer of the article and quotes the statement under attack.

Whereas the first part of the letter deals with particular aspects of the NHS, the rest of the text focuses on more general remarks on the structure of the NHS.

The letter to the editor as a text form is intended to stimulate public discussion on a particular topic of general relevance. The letter writer also aims at modifying an opinion advanced by the editorial staff or other writers. Thus a forum for public discussion and comment on societal developments is established.

11. The Glass Menagerie

1. This text conveys an insight into the social living conditions in America against the background of the thirties and investigates in particular themes and characters in Tennessee Williams' play *The Glass Menagerie*. The text explores in depth the manifold reasons for Laura Wingfield's psychic instability, her final seclusion in a world of her own (see the collection of glass figures), and emphasises the relevance to Williams' recurrent theme of the "inroads of time".

2. In this text themes, events, and characters in Williams' play *The Glass Menagerie* are interpreted by discussing certain facets of the historical situation in America in the thirties and the influence of the playwright's personal experience on the nature of the characters in his plays. Besides these more or less informative elements the text focuses on Laura Wingfield's character and her philosophy of life, which are critically evaluated on the basis of selected quotations from the play. Although the author of the text refrains from evaluations in categories of good or weak, the language itself betrays obvious signs of critical comment (e.g. "this surely is true", l. 4; "surely", l. 9; "it is not improbable to suggest", l. 11). The main intention of this text lies

therefore in passing a personal evaluation of some aspects of the play, thus permitting this text to be classified as 'factional'.

3. This text excerpt reveals a mixture of authorial comment and quotations from the play typical of a coherent text interpretation. In order to balance the analysis and to illustrate and verify the interpretative conclusions, the author also employs references to Williams' life and his complete works. Text interpretation investigates the themes, events, characters and their philosophies of life. It is therefore an attempt at a systematic approach to a text (e.g. structures, historical and biographical backgrounds, literary traditions, the work in the perspective of the writer's œuvre).

The author of a text interpretation thus applies a set of almost conventionalised analytical tools. Text interpretation strives after critical evaluation while revealing a great deal of sound personal assessment. Text interpretation functions to enhance the understanding of fiction and to facilitate the access to writers' works. Moreover, it represents literary criticism intended to stir up academic discourse on particular subjects or writers.

12. The Impact of Energy on Geological Processes

1. This text deals with the different manifestations of energy on, around and inside the planet earth, such as those caused in its atmosphere by the planetary circulation, or on its surface by gravitation, or inside the earth by earthquakes and eruptions of volcanoes, and it names the different scientific disciplines which investigate these forms of energy in terms of their effects on our planet.

2. This text is laden with scientific information and abounds in technical terms which make it difficult for an inexperienced reader to get to grips with. The author provides many definitions and often refers to well-known facts to prove his theoretical statements. There is no personal opinion or evaluation; instead a sober, impartial presentation of facts. For these reasons the text must be classified as non-fictional.

3. This text is one of those scientific reports which aim at presenting objectively verifiable results of scientific investigation in a neutral style in order either to introduce new scientific findings or tentatively propose a new theory or systematize the interrelation of old findings and theories in survey form. The text at hand belongs to the last group in that it tries to divide the field of geological research up into its various subsciences and their respective subjects of investigation. The logical structure follows the

principle *from general to particular* or *from comprehensive to specialized* fields of research. The starting point is always a definition which reveals the main component parts (see, for example, the first sentences of the first four paragraphs), which are then, in turn, subdivided. This text structure can be illustrated in a diagram.

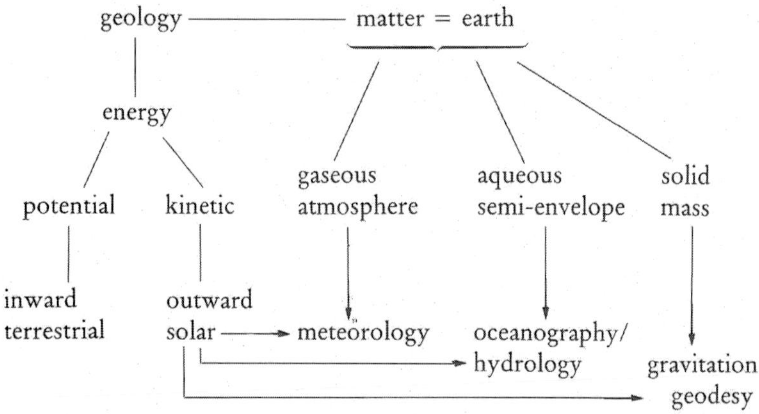

Thus the main characteristics of this text form are logical structure, neutral or technical style, verifiable subject matter, and absence of subjective evaluation.

13. Decision to give Parents Choice...

1. This text is about the British government's decision to give parents the choice as to whether they approve of the cane or not. The criticism brought about following this decision in the groups concerned with its implementation, above all the unequal treatment of children at the same school, is presented in as much detail as the government's reasoning behind this regulation, namely, the wish of many parents and teachers to retain corporal punishment, and the impracticability of a separation into corporal punishment and non-corporal punishment schools.

2. In this text the reader is provided with all kinds of information. There is, firstly, the strictly factual information on the government's decision; the negative consequences it is feared it will have; the official reasons for this decision; and how it is to be implemented. This makes up roughly half of the article (this information is spread over the whole article). The rest is reserved for the personal opinions of the represen-

tatives of the opposing groups, quoted in direct or reported speech. These quotations introduce a departure from the merely factual level of information to a discursive exposition of the problem at hand. Both sides are given about the same space to articulate their views, while the journalist refrains from any subjective evaluation of her own. This attempt at a balanced presentation of opposing views permits one to classify this text as non-fictional.

3. This text is a newspaper report which has the function of presenting facts and events in such a way as to enable the reader to arrive at a critical view without being influenced by the journalist's opinion. Depending on the topic of the report, the stress can be placed differently, either on the facts concerning the outcome of an event; or on the preliminaries or proceedings leading up to a certain outcome; or on the consequences an event might have in the future when put into practice. In this case, the report concentrates on the possible future problems of an event. The quoting of the differing standpoints is the discursive basis for the reader in the process of forming his own opinion. This form of text *seeks* to avoid all authorial subjectivity.

14. Precautions

1. This text gives necessary instructions to be considered when operating a video cassette recorder. The instructions to be followed so as to avoid damage cover proper usage ranging from storage, utilisation, (re-)positioning, transportation and cleaning to special advice on maintenance and service.

2. The operating instructions obviously reflect dimensions of the real world, i.e. the purchase and use of a video cassette recorder. All the instructions given are factual elements and can easily be checked against the reality by simply operating the recorder. One is thus justified in speaking of a one-to-one correspondence of the instructions with the real world. The operating instructions are presented in an extremely informative and expedient manner. They are meant as obligatory directives so as to avoid damage. Although some of the recorder's functions are stressed in positive terms (e.g. "Automatic Moisture Indicator Lamp"), the neutral character of these instructions is by no means affected, thus justifying the classification of this text as non-fictional.

3. This text presents operating instructions intended to enable potential users to operate a video cassette recorder properly, avoiding any mishaps. Each essential aspect of usage is treated in an individual section.

The instructions are formulated in the imperative form, and take on a warning character. The language of these instructions is extremely functional, adequately technical, and lacking in superfluous remarks. The layman has therefore easy access to it.

Operating instructions have various functions such as informing and instructing on the proper use of a product and helping users to avoid misuse, damage and unnecessary repair costs. They are also intended to protect the producer/manufacturer against customers' complaints due to improper use.

15. An Agreement

1. This text determines the conditions under which a cottage is let to a tenant and fixes the terms of payment of the rent.

2. The principal aim of this text is to consider as objectively as possible certain aspects of the real world. The text is strictly informative and every single piece of factual information can be easily checked against the reality. There are, for example, precise details of time and place. The names and addresses of real people, the landlord and the tenant, are stated, and the terms of payment of the rent, the exact date of the first instalment as well as the actual amount, are precisely fixed. Being purely informative, the text strives after accuracy and neutrality and therefore avoids evaluative or even invented elements at all costs. Personal opinion or subjective judgment are nowhere to be found. This attempt at accuracy and objectivity clearly classifies this text as being non-fictional.

3. As an agreement this text belongs to the group of legal documents. Since a legal document is legally binding on all parties involved and enforceable by law, its principal feature is that it has to be as precise as possible in order to avoid ambiguities or the possibility of several interpretations. Therefore a legal document should always be informative, neutral, free of any kind of evaluation or personal judgment, be objective and unambiguous. All these important criteria are to be found in the agreement under discussion.

Chapter II

Text – Structure and Types

1. The Scotty Who Knew Too Much

1. This fable is, amongst other things, all about the arrogance with which city dwellers treat country people because of the latters' alleged ignorance. In this particular fable the pretensions of the urban Scotty are severely punished on three occasions.

2. The first two sentences constitute the introduction. The time and place of action are only vaguely hinted at in the first sentence, but for the purposes of the plot it is only necessary to know that the scene is set in the country. The next sentence points out the central opposition between the arrogant know-all, Scotty, from the city and the allegedly stupid farm dog from the country, who has no name. In his first words the Scotty also makes clear what he is about to do to prove his own superiority, thus preparing the action of the following part. The middle section comprises the rest of the text, excluding only the moral. In a climatic arrangement it presents the Scotty's three fights and three defeats. These three episodes show a strictly parallel structure. They all start with a brief conversation between the two dogs (Scotty: statement/command – farm dog: question – Scotty: negative answer/command) followed by the action (way to the animal and the fights); the verbal analysis of each fight; and, where relevant, medical treatment. Though the opponents appear less dangerous in these fights, the wounds they inflict become severer, and the Scotty finally ends up in a city hospital. The moral forms, by convention, the final part of the fable and supplies a witty conclusion to the events of the text. Or, to put it another way, the moral contains the quintessence of a story or episode which functions as its illustration.

3. This text is predominantly narrative, the stress being placed on action rather than description. Only the moral can be categorised otherwise, as it instructively suggests how to behave wisely.

2. Early Autumn

1. This text is about a man and a woman who were in love once and meet by chance after years of having heard nothing from each other. The long separation has made the former lovers, in the meantime both married and with families of their own, strangers to each other who do not have anything in common any more. They are not able to exchange more than

mere superficialities. On his part there is only cold and distant politeness, whereas she seems to regret their separation; they separate after a few minutes without even exchanging their addresses.

2. The first paragraph of this short story constitutes the exposition preparing for the main section by narrating prior events and facts and introducing the two characters. The vague information is revealed that the two characters were in love once but separated after a quarrel about some trifling matter. Apart from relating prior events this exposition hints at the fact that Mary might not really love the man she married ("... a man she thought she loved"). This impression is reinforced in the middle and final sections.

The middle section consists of about three quarters of the text (except the last paragraph). In chronological order Bill's and Mary's short encounter is related from their chance meeting to their farewell a few minutes later, which forms the end of the middle section. The function of this text section is to show the nature of their relationship after years of separation. In this context several things are of importance: the awkwardness of the meeting and the estrangement of old friends; the superficiality of the conversation and Bill's distant politeness; the fact that Mary's love for Bill has not died. The clues that she is still in love with Bill or at least regrets their separation form a contrasting pattern to Bill's distant behaviour ("she lifted her face as though wanting a kiss"; "... desperately reaching back into the past"; "'When...' she wanted to say").

The structural pattern of the middle section is characterized by an alternation of dialogue and reflective passages on Mary's part. Thus a strong contrast between the exchange of polite and meaningless phrases and Mary's deeper thoughts and feeling, which, however, she is not able to express, is formed emphasizing the estrangement of Bill and Mary. The description of autumn mood (ll. 33/4) symbolically sums up Mary's physical and emotional state.

The final section, consisting of the last paragraph, forms the climax of the text by Mary's sudden but nevertheless belated realization that she did not ask the important things she wanted to and the fact that she still loves Bill, which is revealed by the name of her youngest son.

3. Since this short story concentrates solely on the short encounter of the former lovers and therefore relates the conversation, reflexion, and action during that meeting, this constituting the plot, there is an almost complete predominance of the narrative text type. There are only very few and short descriptive elements to be found, e.g. "The leaves fell slowly from the trees in the Square. Fell without wind. Autumn dusk."

3. How can she be happy

1. This poem is about the disturbed relationship between a husband and wife who blame each other for being the source of their respective unhappiness.

2. This poem can be divided up into either two or three sense units. The first stanza can be seen as an introduction to the subject central to the poem, namely, the possibility or rather impossibility of being happy when one's partner is not. Time and place of action are not mentioned; nor are the characters described in any detail or specifically referred to by name. This is an indication that the subject is generally applicable and not to be merely individualised. The following four stanzas form the middle section and develop the arguments of both sides in an antithetical or contrastive fashion. The man, in a kind of frame, is given the first and last words, while the woman's arguments are contained in the middle. There is a certain symmetry in the text in that the woman is given two stanzas of five lines each, whereas the man also has two stanzas, but with only three lines to them; this is, of course, excluding the last line, which consists of only one word, significantly indicating the poem's subject of happiness (or lack of it). There is no real solution to the problem, unless one takes the last stanza as the conclusion. From the compositional point of view this would not appear to be logical, though on the content level some evidence can be given in support of this division. All the stanzas deal with the interplay of feelings between the man and woman and the mutual interdependence of their reactions. In the final stanza, however, the man is only concerned with himself, and the conclusions he comes to are self-centred. This egocentricity is also expressed by the italicising of the word 'He' at the beginning of the last stanza. The apparent contradiction between composition (parallelism; no solution) and content (man thinking of himself alone) is not necessarily a sign of poetic inadequacy but perhaps an attempt to suggest a feasible solution or at least understanding of the problem without forcing it unduly upon the reader.

3. This poem is an argumentative text in that two conflicting standpoints are contrasted, in this case the two opposed views on who is to blame for the unhappiness prevalent in a relationship. As has already been pointed out, no explicit evaluation is given.

4. Vintage Stuff

1. This text very concisely describes the development of a boy from his birth, in this context also presenting details about his parents, to the age of nine when his general behaviour at home and at school is still exceptionally good.

2. This text is an excerpt from the introductory chapter of a novel. Nevertheless it should be treated as an independent and self-contained unit.

The text can be divided into three parts. The first part consists of the first four paragraphs, which introduce the main character, Peregrine Roderick Clyde-Browne, and his parents, provide information about his family background, about the baby and his reception by hospital staff and his parents, and about his development from early infancy to the age of nine when his principal characteristic is still his unusually good behaviour. It schould be noted that there is a large discrepancy between narrative time and narrated time as the relevant information about the characters and a lapse of nine years are set forth in four short paragraphs. Due to this concentration on a few important facts there is an almost complete predominance of narrative passages in the first part.

A strong contrast is formed by the second part of the text, the dialogue between Mr. and Mrs. Clyde-Browne, where an almost one-to-one correspondence between narrative time and narrated time can be found. In contrast to the first part the second part concentrates on a very short period of time relating one short but significant dialogue.

The third part of this text, which is formed by the last paragraph, returns to the method employed in the first part. A relatively long period of time, one year, is covered in one short paragraph. The development of this text is a movement from a drastically shortened period of time in the first part to the concentration on one particular point of time in the second part and back to a shortened period of time in the third part.

3. With the exception of one descriptive sentence ("Peregrine's beauty was of the sort usually seen after a particularly nasty car accident.") this text is characterized by an exclusive use of narrative elements. The reason for this predominance lies in the intention of this text, which narrates facts and prior events in order to characterize the main character.

5. New Lamps for Old

1. This text explores the opportunities for a sensible approach towards societal developments, neglecting the futile dualism between progress and conservatism. The author emphasises the continued relevance of the traditional balance between old achievements and modern inventions and argues for a compromise between a materialistic perspective and cultural values (e.g. aesthetics, ethics).

2. Although this text is an excerpt from an essay, it is considered here as an independent text. This text can be divided into either two or three sections. The introduction comprises the first two paragraphs, in which the author specifies the difficulties of his approach ("it is not easy to make a case for any sort of conservation") due to the futile dualism between tradition and innovation in social developments. The introduction leads on to the middle section, which comprises the rest of the text (this approach will be pursued here), and it seems also justifiable to regard the last two sentences ("After all...) as a conclusion. The text's main section is particularly devoted to the formation of the author's own position, rejecting extreme standpoints such as reckless progress on the one hand or anxious conservation on the other. First of all he proposes to overcome the pointless dichotomy between innovation and conservation and supports this standpoint with an example from modern architecture (fourth paragraph). Then he comments on approaches intended to modify a purely materialistic attitude towards life by claiming some significance of "the spiritual". The comprehensive discussion of the set problem in the text's main section is concluded by the author advocating the necessity of a free and thriving human spirit, also pointing out some negative consequences of its absence (concentration camps, suppression of critical comment). Thus the author develops his own position by contrasting extreme approaches to the problem of social developments.

3. This text is a predominantly argumentative text, concentrating mainly on a discussion of conflicting standpoints on a particular problem. Although there are some expository elements in the presentation of these standpoints, the author's principal intention is to "make a case for", or, in other words, to substantiate his idea of conservation.

6. Proud to be British

1. This text is devoted to an inquiry into the changing attitudes of British people towards patriotism which are particularly evident in the views of

today's intellectuals and writers in England. On the occasion of the fortieth anniversary of D-day, an international survey was carried out revealing that the majority of the Britons are still "proud to be British".

2. This text forms the introduction to a comprehensive report on an international survey about patriotism. It is nevertheless possible to distinguish three sections in this text. In the first two paragraphs historically changing attitudes among the general public are stated. The theme discussed is enriched by contradictory quotations from some of England's most famous writers (second paragraph). The function of these introductory paragraphs is to present the subject of the survey and it explains its topicality by referring to D-day. Moreover, this change in attitudes is introduced with a certain degree of erudition.

The middle section, introduced by the contrastive "but", concentrates on today's situation and reports on details of the survey carried out such as the polling institute, the conditions of the survey, the people interviewed, and the kind of questions. Thus this text section prepares for the detailed results provided in the third section, which reveals the degree to which the Britons are still proud of their nationality. This section therefore illustrates the initial problem by presenting verifiable data. It also conveys a preliminary impression on the outcome of the survey's results. As might have become clear from the analysis, this text moves from general observations on patriotism in the first section to details of the conditions of the survey in the second section on to particular results of the survey in the final section. Whereas the first section and part of the second section are organised antithetically (yet, but), the second section also lists the survey conditions as does the third section with regard to the results of the survey. The final section also gives the answer to the initial questions.

3. This text is both argumentative and expository as it relates ideas on patriotism from a traditional and a modern perspective, and presents the views of both "the intellectuals and writers of England" and the ordinary people. In the main, however, the text reports on the empirical data of the survey on patriotism; in this section the text is expository.

7. Real Kids vs. 'The Average' Family

1. This text is about the changes in the American family, i.e. the unmistakable development towards single-parent families. The educa-

tional system and the mass media, however, fail to reflect this reality and still stick to the conventional 'myths'.

2, This text is the introduction to an article on the structure of the American family. It is most likely that pupils will analyse the three paragraphs which make up this text in terms of introduction, middle section, and conclusion (as of course intended), as they must necessarily treat the text as a self-contained unit. This approach will be pursued here, too.

The first paragraph points out the general significance of the subject and the public attention it has already aroused. The second paragraph focuses on one specific example to demonstrate the individual problems involved as a result of the fundamental changes in family life. The third paragraph returns to the general level and denounces the persistent adherence to out-dated concepts in connection with the family, concepts responsible for the feeling children have "of not quite fitting". The argumentation moves from the general to the particular and back to the general; in other words, the general introduction is followed by a specific example in the middle section and by a preliminary conclusion in general terms in the final paragraph.

3. This text has to be classified as an expository text which sets out to analyse the traditional and contemporary concepts linked to the composition of the American family. The example contains certain narrative elements which are, however, subordinate to the purpose of developing a coherent theoretical analysis.

8. Bringing up Mother

1. This text is about the interrelation between parents and children, i.e. about the way in which they influence and mould each other in a process of mutuality and not, as has commonly been accepted, in a one-way process, with the parents educating and shaping their children.

2. This text is the beginning of a longer article, but will be dealt with as a complete unit in itself (see note on previous text). It can be divided up into three sections. The first two paragraphs, which serve as the first step in the argumentation rather than as the introduction, present two case studies of mother-child relationships. These contrasting examples, illustrations from experience, serve as the basis of the theoretical conclusions in this text. The next step in the argumentation (third paragraph) gives factual evidence enabling one to rule out the view that the differences are the effect of the mothers' personalities or their living conditions. The

third step, the conclusion, comprises the following two paragraphs. In the fourth paragraph the answer is given and underlined by factual evidence gained through observation. The last paragraph integrates these findings into a broader theoretical framework concerning parent-child relationships, stressing in particular the reciprocity of influences. In this form the argumentation moves from the presentation of effects as seen in everyday life to the investigation of their causes and the formulation of a theoretical conclusion.

3. This text is an expository text. A new theory concerning the parent-child relationship is developed in a logically convincing way. The last paragraph, by contrasting two different standpoints, also contains elements of the argumentative text type, but this is not a predominant feature, as the one angle is not discussed in any detail.

9. Take 5

1. This text deals with the various factors a teacher of a foreign language has to consider when deciding to use a game in language classes, namely the aim of the game, the students' interest, and when to use a game, to provide an opportunity for students to use their language skills in a less formal situation.

2. This text is part of a longer introduction but should of course be dealt with as a self-contained text unit. It can be divided into three main sections: an introductory section, a middle section, and a final section.

The first paragraph constitutes the introduction, which presents the theme of the text in the form of a general statement or thesis. It states that there are many factors to be taken into account to make the use of a language game a success. The first sentence serves as an introduction whereas the incomplete second sentence links the introduction to the middle section. This is achieved by naming one of the factors to be considered and at the same time indicating that there are other important factors.

These factors are listed in the middle section which comprises three paragraphs. These enumerated paragraphs show a parallel structure, each paragraph dealing with one important factor; the respective factor under discussion is presented in a general question. Then these general factors are explained in some detail to show the complexity of the problem. Thus the argumentation within these three paragraphs moves from the general to the particular.

The final section consists of the last paragraph. The first sentence takes the form of a conclusion but also gives further instructions for the teacher. The consideration of the different factors dealt with in the middle section is regarded as a basic requirement for any qualified choice of an appropriate game. Thus middle section and conclusion are linked together. However, there are also other things to be taken into account. Again the argumentation moves from the general instruction of the first sentence (the choice of a game should only be confirmed if it is feasible in the classroom) to the particular in the second sentence by explaining this instruction in detail. The internal composition of the middle and final sections is characterized by the move from the general to the particular. The interrelation between the text sections, however, can be described as a move from the general introduction to the particular in the middle section back to the general in the final section.

3. This is a predominantly expository text as it sets forth the various factors to be considered for the right language game in class in a step-by-step fashion in the introductory and the middle sections. The final section, however, gives instructions for the language teacher and therefore has to be classified as instructive.

10. Battle of Trafalgar

1. This text on the Battle of Trafalgar not only describes in detail how Nelson defeated Villeneuve, but also refers briefly to the historical significance of this victory.

2. This text can be divided up into four sections. The first paragraph constitutes the introduction and presents in short the most important facts and consequences of this battle: time and place, number of ships in each fleet, names of admirals, resultant duration of British naval supremacy. The second paragraph, which together with the first half of the third forms the middle section, describes the events on the Spanish side prior to the battle. The first half of the third paragraph then gives a detailed chronological survey of the proceedings during the actual battle itself. The second half, in the manner of a conclusion, cites the number of casualties and material losses on both sides; and the last sentence again points out the broader significance of this battle for Britain. The purpose of this text is to supply the reader with concise and accurate information (even though a hint of patriotism cannot be overlooked. See Nelson's message).

3. This text is a predominantly narrative text concentrating on events and actions rather than on description or argumentation. The conclusions that are drawn, however, go beyond the dimensions of mere narration and tend towards an expository approach.

Chapter III

Point of View

1. Tom Jones

1. This text is written from the point of view of a first person omniscient narrator, i.e. someone who does not himself participate in the action, but observes from the outside and evaluates from above the characters and events he chooses to present. The omniscient narrator has free access to his material, and in this excerpt he emphatically announces his intention to exploit this situation. A direct characterisation of the narrator is not possible for the obvious reason that there is no one apart from himself in a position to do so. In this passage the narrator reveals a certain degree of learning and arrogance in the way he places his own aesthetic standards beyond the reach of any criticism. By the way he directly addresses the reader at the very beginning of this text it is made clear that the reader is not granted the right to judge. The narrator also shows a kind of social snobbishness in classifying all poor people as idle beggars.

2. It becomes obvious in this text extract that the reader is completely at the mercy of the omniscient narrator. This holds true not only for the course of events, which the narrator can interfere with at will, but also for the presentation of his own character and faculties. The effect can be seen as a 'spoon-feeding' of the reader, who may resent the frequent authorial interruptions, as the narrator seeks to make up the reader's mind for him. The reader is reduced to a mere consumer of literature and is made acutely aware of his restricted role by the overwhelming presence of the narrator. This guidance can, of course, also be accepted by the reader as useful for his reception of the novel, especially if his own aesthetic and social attitudes correspond with those of the narrator. By unfolding the principles according to which the novel is composed the narrator conveys theoretical knowledge not normally provided by a piece of literature and which could help the reader in his evaluation of the work.

2. Plants

1. This text is written from the point of view of a third-person omniscient narrator who gives advice on how to look after plants. These pieces of advice take the form of imperatives directed at the reader, followed by

general statements which should not be contradicted and which serve as back-up evidence. The reader is not provided with a full line of argumentation but has to accept the narrator's opinion solely on the basis of the latter's authority. The narrator reveals nothing about his own character; it is obvious, however, that he must be an expert on household plants.

2. The direct and close relationship between narrator and reader is made clear by the many imperatives used in this text. This relationship is, however, one-sided in that the reader is told categorically what to do should he wish to be successful in his gardening venture. In this case the reader will not resent the narrator's dominant role because the reason for consulting a text of this kind is due to the reader's own lack of knowledge on the subject and his wish to find expert advice to compensate for this information deficit. The peremptory tone and the almost impersonal brevity and conciseness of the commands contribute rather to the accuracy and reliability of the advice given than putting the reader off reading on.

3. Romeo and Juliet

1. The prologue of *Romeo and Juliet* provides the reader with a brief plot outline of the play and aims at increasing the tension and heightening the reader's attention and anticipation. The text is written from the point of view of a first-person omniscient narrator. In accordance with the conventional use of the chorus in drama it does not participate in the action, but in an extremely concise manner evaluates from above the events and characters it presents. The narrator reveals nothing of his own character. A direct characterisation of the narrator is impossible and unnecessary, because he remains outside the plot and it is his task to provide the reader with information. The narrator directly addresses the reader to prepare him for what is going to come next, i.e. the performance of the play.

2. Though the reader depends on the information and evaluation given by the narrator, i.e. he is guided in his expectations, he is not completely at the narrator's mercy. This is made clear in the narrator's direct address to the reader: "... if you with patient ears attend, what here shall miss, our toil shall strive to mend." Though at this stage the reader completely depends on the narrator's judgment, he will have the opportunity to check the latter's reliability.

By only providing a rough outline and commentary of the plot the narrator does not make use of his absolute authority. This lessens the feeling on the reader's part of complete guidance by a 'know-all' narrator considerably.

4. Sense and Sensibility

1. This text excerpt is written from the point of view of a third person omniscient narrator. The narrator does not himself participate in the action but is endowed with the power of complete insight into his characters' thoughts, emotions, and motivations. He thus views his characters from outside and provides the reader with his comments and evaluations. He evaluates Mr. John Dashwood's character, that of his wife, and Mr. Dashwood's intentions concerning the provision of his sisters. Every single item of information given to the reader is already interpreted by the omniscient narrator, who supplies his knowledge and comments as he thinks fit. Though the presentation of the protagonist's thoughts in the second half of the second paragraph seems to take the form of reported thought, it is really a direct presentation of his thoughts, because the reader does not follow the events through the eyes of the protagonist but is directed by the omniscient narrator. This method is used to pretend to the reader a close relationship between himself and the protagonist. He is, however, completely guided, influenced, and manipulated by the narrator.

2. The advantage of the point of view adopted in this text lies in the narrator's total access to his characters' motivations, feelings, and thoughts and therefore in his ability to present the subtle mental processes and developments of any character he chooses. The obvious disadvantage of this point of view, however, lies in the narrator's overwhelming dominance, which severely restricts the reader's range of possibilities by providing him with ready-made opinions and evaluations and by trying to direct his judgment in a way predetermined by the 'know-all' narrator. The reader has no chance to find out certain facts and meanings for himself, but is reduced to a very passive and receptive role.

5. The Loneliness of the Long-Distance Runner

1. The point of view adopted in this text can be classified as first person central consciousness. The narrator, who is identical with the story's

main protagonist (narrator-protagonist), soliloquises on why he has ended up in a borstal and what happens to him in there. This report from the first person perspective transcends the limits of self-centredness in that there are some direct addresses to the reader intended to intensify the relationship between narrator and reader. In a thematically consistent manner the narrator reveals the reasons for his present predicament, how he came to be occupied with long-distance running, his attitude towards getting away from the borstal, his view of the borstal officers, and what – according to him – counts in life. These events, experiences, and opinions are viewed and related (note the informal quality of the language) through the narrator's eyes and thus convey an understanding of his state of mind. The narrator presents himself in a know-all and precocious manner as a self-confident person, admittedly not without a sense of the comic (see the pun on long-distance running). This self-presentation, however, by no means offers an objective insight into his personality, and this also holds true for his biased evaluation of the other characters, i.e. the borstal officers. They are described in rather derogatory terms (e.g. them bastards), as the narrator knows their craftiness in dealing with offenders.

2. The choice of a first person central consciousness point of view guides the reader's response to a text in many ways. This point of view dispenses with a mediator who relates the protagonist's experience(s) to the reader; in other words, there is a coincidence of narrator and protagonist. Thus the reader follows the current course of events and the narrator's retrospection and reflexion through the latter's eyes and experiences the story with a great deal of immediacy. As a result, the reader is confronted with a protagonist-centred and highly subjective presentation and evaluation of events, characters, and ideas in the story (note the recurrent first person singular). The reader is also liable to be influenced depending on the degree of his identification with the narrator. In this text the narrator establishes a close relationship to the reader by directly addressing him; this facilitates the reader's access to the story, although it makes it difficult for him to take a critical stance towards the text's events, characters, ideas and the narrator's value judgments.

The obvious limitations of this point of view lie in its lack of a variety of standpoints which could put the narrator-protagonist's words into perspective. The emerging narrator bias may take such forms as unreliable reports, distortion and concealment of facts, exaggeration and understatement.

6. A Visit of Charity

1. This opening of a short story is told from the point of view of a third person central consciousness, i.e. the narrator is the protagonist of the story. From the start the reader gets all the information and impressions filtered through Marian's mind; as a result there is no objectivity of judgment and no distance to or detachment from the events. The effect is a closeness between reader and protagonist which, in this case, is illustrated in the use of reported thought ("How dark it was!"). The reader is not provided with any direct characterisation of the narrator, as Marian does not reflect on herself nor does she relate what others think of her. Instead the reader has to infer everything from the way she perceives and describes her environment, above all from the comparisons she uses ("like the interior of a clock", "like a sheep bleating", "quick as a bird claw", "like being caught in a robbers' cave"). Her vivid imagination recreates her naivety and inexperience, which can either completely win the reader over or make him smile a smile of superiority.

2. The advantage of this point of view lies particularly in the immediacy with which the reader is able to follow the course of events. His response is most probably an identification with the protagonist, whose state of mind is witnessed by the reader from within the protagonist-narrator's mind. It is, however, difficult for the reader to judge the reliability of this presentation. His task, therefore, is to find out whether the narrator conveys a valid description of the events outside her own mind or whether this description merely reflects her psyche. The reader's role is an active one as he has to decide to what extent his initial spontaneous identification with the narrator can be justified on emotional or rational grounds.

7. A Portrait of the Artist as a Young Man

1. This text is written from the point of view of a third person central consciousness. Throughout the passage the narrator-protagonist reflects on himself through the medium of reported thought. Only the second sentence contains a piece of factual description. The narrator imagines his own death and the reactions this would cause, especially in someone by the name of Wells. Consequently there can be no direct characterisation of the narrator by anyone else. In his fantasies he reveals himself as full of ineffectual self-pity together with a touch of complacency, as someone who resents being slighted or wronged. His escape into the illusive world

of his imagination is perhaps a pointer to his actual significance or his incapacity to solve his problems in real life.

2. The reader becomes the confidant of the narrator, whose thoughts he shares and whose mental development he experiences without any interference or mediation. An identification is almost inevitable, and this can result in two different responses in the reader. He may either sympathise with the narrator or even partly recognize himself in him, a recognition which will make him follow the events with pleasure and approval. Or he may reject his behaviour and disapprove of his reactions, a response which must necessarily cause a feeling of antipathy in the course of reading, as there is no escape from the narrator. Even if the reader likes the plot or wit of the narration, he will hardly be able to relish them as the dominance of the narrator is total.

8. A Tradition of Eighteen Hundred and Four

1. The narrator of this opening of a short story describes the events from the point of view of a first person minor character. The narrator does not himself take an active part in the action but is an unimportant character who views everything from the stance of a witness on the periphery. The reader scarcely gets any information about the narrator. Though he acts as a mediator between the reader and Solomon Selby's story, the narrator's relation to the story and the reader is confined to that of a witness whose prime and only task is to report. Therefore he is hardly characterised. He does not try to influence the reader or to evaluate the event of the story. His position as a witness who refrains from any interference is emphasized by the fact that Solomon Selby's story is presented in direct speech and takes up the rest of the short story. The witness only reappears at the very end.

2. The advantage of this point of view is that the reader is provided with information without being influenced by any subjective evaluations given by the narrator. He can listen to the story and come to his own conclusions without being guided by any ready-made opinions. Thus the narrator bias is reduced to a minimum. It is left to the reader to find out if the narrator's report is reliable.

The limitations of this point of view are in some respects similar to those of an eliminated narrator. Since the narrator views and evaluates everything at face value as a witness who does not himself participate in the action the range of reflexion, for example, can only be related if perceptible in outward appearance or action.

9. Royal Praise, Martina's Day

1. These texts completely dispense with an identifiable narrator; the point of view adopted here can be classified as the eliminated narrator. *Royal Praise* relates the protagonists (i.e. the Queen, the Boys' Brigade), the occasion of the honour (centenary celebration of the brigade), as well as the time and place of the ceremony in an extremely concise manner. This also applies to *Martina's Day*, a text which also names the protagonists (i.e. M. Navratilova, A. Jaeger), the occasion of the match (Wimbledon women's singles final), the result, the winner, and the prize. Although the events in both texts are regarded as remarkable (the Queen's royal review) and exceptional (M. Navratilova's walkover victory), the narrator is practically absent and would seem to have no insight into the characters and events or any close relation to them. Hence the narrator refrains from interfering with value judgments; and it is totally left up to the reader to derive any significance from the events reported on and to decide on the legitimacy of their assumed noteworthiness.

2. The choice of an eliminated narrator point of view has manifold effects on the reader's relation to the text. Due to the absence of a meddling narrator, the characters, setting, and events are revealed in a very to-the-point manner. Although these texts contain some evaluative qualifications regarding the remarkable nature of the events, these texts do not provide the reader with ready-made authorial opinion. As the reader is hardly guided and influenced in his reception of these texts, this point of view allows the reader the advantage of evaluating characters and events unswayed by authorial bias. The reader, although he is forced to make an interpretative effort, is free to develop his personal understanding of the text's characters and events. This point of view encourages the reader, as it were, to express original thought and to assess the message, the essence, and the evaluation to be found in these texts. The limitation of this point of view is the absence of a narrator who explains events and characters, clarifies ambiguities, and provides the reader with moral values as well as authorial support in his reception of a text.

10. Hills like White Elephants

1. This short story opening does not reveal the presence of a narrator, limited or unlimited. The first paragraph contains the description of the actual surroundings without comment or evaluation. The section that follows shows the dialogue between the two protagonists, again pre-

sented neutrally, without authorial interference. This dialogue is only interrupted by information concerning the action ("The woman brought two glasses of beer...") and details of the physical environment ("They were white in the sun and the country was brown and dry.") The reader is in the position of an observer, at a distance, forming his own opinion on the basis of the surface information given.

2. The unquestionable advantage of doing without a narrator lies in the freedom it gives the reader. Without the meddling of a 'know-all' narrator the reader has to find out for himself the meaning of certain passages and how the overall message is to be interpreted. The limitations of this point of view lie in the respective modes of presentation. Only neutral description and dialogue are possible, i.e. only the view from outside is compatible with this approach. Any references to subtle mental processes not reflected in outward actions or reactions have to be left out. This may be the reason why this point of view is found mostly in short or action-based narratives which do not require phases of reflection or analyses of character development.

11. New Year's Deadly Night of Panic

1. This newspaper report shows a mixed point of view (shifting perspective). The main report on the events in Trafalgar Square during the New Year's Eve celebrations 1982 is factual and aims at objectivity, but also contains some kind of generally accepted criticism as to the co-operation of the bodies responsible. Thus the prevailing perspective is that of the eliminated narrator. This text also comprises first-hand statements (direct and reported speech) from people present in the square, e.g. the London Ambulance Spokesman and so-called "others in the square". These witnesses comment from a limited perspective on how the disaster came about, namely, on the stampede and the subsequent deaths of two women, from their personal observation. They can therefore be classified as minor characters on the periphery, who characterise themselves through their statements. In the context of the witnesses' different experiences and relation to the events in the square, their observations and explanations on the causes of the disaster and on those responsible also vary. The text is therefore classified on the basis of a fact-based report from the eliminated narrator perspective and by the conflicting statements of the witnesses from their limited points of view.

2. The shifting perspective to be found in this text combines the advantages of an eliminated narrator perspective (attempt at factuality

and an objective reconstruction of reality, abstaining from authorial interference) with those of a limited perspective (the dramatic and immediate quality of a witness's personal experience). The general mood of uncertainty and fragmentary knowledge about the causes of the disaster is reflected in the eliminated narrator perspective chosen in this text. This point of view provides a 'summarising' review of the incidents from an outside standpoint, whereas the witnesses' reports overcome these limitations allowing at least a restricted personal insight into the possible causes of the tragedy. With the help of a number of standpoints, an objective report is intended. The reader is not guided in his response to the text, but is left with the task or freedom to establish his own pattern of the true nature of the catastrophe. He is not influenced in the way he forms his personal view on the probability and significance of the witnesses' statements, though he is forced to accept facts such as the time of the tragedy, medical treatment of the victims, and the identification of the dead.

12. Macbeth

1. In this text the reader is not confronted with a narrator but with the characters, who present themselves without authorial intervention. First the reader is given a report in a letter written, as is convention, in the first person. Then he witnesses the reaction of the receiver, who comments on the writer's character, again in the first person. These two subjective views not only illustrate the same event from two different angles, but also reveal the relationship between the two characters and what they think of each other; and, perhaps more importantly, what kind of characters they have (Macbeth: ambitious yet wavering in his aspirations; Lady Macbeth: ruthless in the pursuit of her aims). The splitting-up of the task of presentation (a technique most frequently and effectively employed in the field of drama) thus provides an abundance of information within a relatively small space.

2. The main advantage of this method is that it combines two events otherwise separated by time and place by making use of the letter as a means of conveying messages. Lady Macbeth becomes, as it were, an additional witness of the witches' prophecies. In the absence of her husband she is given the chance to comment openly, an opportunity which would not be possible in that form in a direct confrontation. For the reader this implies an additional means of judging the characters of the protagonists, who, unawares, expose their inner feelings and attitudes, as they feel unobserved.

13. The Lapse

1. The central character, through whose eyes all the events are presented, is Henry, who takes his morning journey to work as an opportunity to reflect on his life and its monotony. He is obviously tired of his daily routine, in which nothing ever seems to change. Only the train moves, but there, too, we find monotony in the steady "ra-ta-ta", in the calculable slowing-down and accelerating, its route dictated by the rails on which it travels. Henry's existence is also completely determined by external factors; he, too, has become predictable, even in the evening when he might have the chance to break away from his routine – he is at a loss as to what to do with himself ("I don't know what to do, I can never make up my mind."). He knows that he is "condemned to serve a lifer" and seemingly submits to his fate in resignation.

2. The point of view of central consciousness chosen in this text has the advantage that the reader knows exactly what is going on in the main character's mind. In this way a close relationship is established between reader and narrator, sometimes to the point of identification. In this excerpt access to the protagonist's thoughts is accomplished in several ways. The text starts with a normal third person central consciousness perspective for the description of the situation when entering the train. When Henry starts to ponder on his life the perspective is altered to that of an interior monologue ("how many times have I done this journey..."). The use of the first-person singular "I" brings Henry closer to the reader and creates sympathy for his feeble attempt to escape the monotony of his life. The description of the journey leads back to the third person perspective. The last three lines again offer a direct insight into Henry's mind, and again this shift is introduced by a question. In contrast to the first occasion, however, this question is a combination of a direct question and a main clause normally only found in reported speech ("What shall I do tonight, the tired voice asked in his head."). These varying degrees of insight into Henry's mind and psyche create tension in the reader, whose reactions towards the central character are never static but vary from close proximity and sympathy to a certain aloofness and pity.

14. Ulysses

1. This text extract is written from a first-person central consciousness point of view. The narrator-protagonist (Mrs. Bloom) would seem to be

recalling certain past events, i.e. when staying with her husband at the City Arms Hotel. The narrative technique of stream of consciousness employed in this text makes it necessary to summarise and reconstruct the events at the hotel from the narrator-protagonist's recollection, which is very much devoid of punctuation and a comprehensible syntax structure: Mrs. Bloom's husband fakes an illness to start off an affair with Mrs. Riordan, who emerges as a great miser and a very talkative hypocrite. Mr. Riordan, apparently a polite person, seems to enjoy some leave from his wife. Mr. Bloom is considered a hypochondriac full of self-pity, and also very open to other women's advances. Most of the events reported on and characters presented are full of mainly derogatory evaluation. The narrator-protagonist's perspective prevails, and the text conveys the impact of the City Arms days on Mrs. Bloom's mind. These recollections lack a coherent structure and have a very associative quality. The narrator-protagonist appears as someone very dissatisfied both with herself and the situation around her. This inner state is articulated in her almost caustic comments on the other characters, except Mr. Riordan. The main target of her harsh criticism is in fact her husband with his tendency to dramatise his ailments and to make himself attractive to other women such as Mrs. Riordan and Miss Stack, a habit arousing the narrator-protagonist's jealousy.

2. In this text, because of the stream of consciousness technique, the reader acquires a detailed insight into the narrator-protagonist's private world and into her psychic condition. He gets very much involved in the way the narrator-protagonist responds to the events at the City Arms Hotel and to the other guests staying at this place. Thus a very intimate relationship is established between the narrator and the reader in which the reader becomes well informed about Mrs. Bloom's thoughts, motivations, likes and dislikes. There is, however, a limiting factor in this technique in that no objectifying point of view is to be found in the extract. That is to say, the narrator-protagonist's assessment of events and characters dominates and the reader can hardly go beyond Mrs. Bloom's subjective grasp of the outside reality. The chosen technique allows the reader to experience Mrs. Bloom's associative recollections with a great deal of immediacy and closeness. In this context the reader's identification with the narrator-protagonist does not seem likely, although the reader can respond either with sympathy or rejection. This response depends largely on the degree of reliability the reader assigns to the narrator-protagonist's statements.

Chapter IV

Plot and Characters

1. Chips with Everything

1. Corporal Hill is presented as a man who completely identifies with the military rules and regulations ("The R.A.F. brought me up."). He is the conscious and proud embodiment of a kind of authority that carries with it the possibility of physically and mentally wrecking the trainee soldiers ("some of you will break down"). The honour of the army/air force sets the ultimate standard of behaviour, and any violation is severely punished ("But I will tear and mercilessly scratch..."). The offer of fairness is only made in the case of complete submission to and execution of Hill's wishes.

2. Hill characterises himself in his speech to the new conscripts, partly through what he says (see answer 1) and partly through the way he conveys his message. He talks about himself in very short sentence units, mostly in the form of parataxis (the juxtaposition of clauses in a sentence without the use of a conjunction), and simple statements. To emphasise the message he wants to get across he sometimes repeats parts of sentences ("It's in a state now, ... so it's in a state now." "But I'll play fair. You do me proud and I'll play fair."), or uses questions that directly address the conscripts ("Is that understood?" "This billet here, you see it?"). A striking feature is the frequent use of slang expressions, some of them vulgar. All this characterises Hill as a man of low social standing and inferior education whose strong desire for authority and power is based on his position in the army rather than on his human or intellectual qualities. He symbolises the hollowness of military structures and ranks which do not match individual capacities but rely on the willingness of the individual to renounce his personal views and opinions in favour of army ritual and subordination in order to be able to exercise power over others. The effectiveness of this method of characterisation by the character himself through language lies in the fact that much more is revealed than is directly expressed or than the person involved is aware of. The lack of human relationships between officers and men is clearly demonstrated by the use of words implying corporal punishment, even while fair play and sympathy are offered. And one is left in hardly any doubt that words alluding to corporal punishment are not the only deterrent, but that punishment itself could follow.

2. Personal Column, Requests for Friendship

1. What the three women and three men have in common is that they want to find a partner, presumably for a number of reasons; for example, because they are divorced or because they do not seem to have anyone to share their lives with. The most frequent components that make up these self-characterisations are age (5 out of 6), profession (all 3 women, but only 1 man), pastimes (4), family or marital status (3), character (3), and political leanings (2). A reference of some sort is always made to the place of residence. The sought-after partner is described according to characteristic features (4/5), age (3), pastimes (2), looks (2), intellect (1), and smoking habits (1). A more detailed characterisation is not possible as there is only space for a few telling words.

2. In an advertisement in a personal column the confined space available makes a focusing on the most important characteristics and revelations necessary and unavoidable. The writer can characterise himself firstly by directly giving information about himself and secondly, indirectly, by enumerating the qualities he expects in his or her partner. However, because the text has to be reduced to references to allegedly important character traits, this often leads to disappointments at the partners' first meeting, when the information proves inadequate or, even worse, turns out to be totally inaccurate, the writer's opinion of him- or herself being immodestly and untruthfully flattering. The degree of abstractness (due to the forced brevity of the text form) of these ads makes it almost impossible to acquire a fair impression of what kind of person to expect.

3. The Mysterious Affair at Styles

1. The character we learn most about is Poirot even though he is not the narrator. All we can say about the narrator is that he is obviously confused by events ("I was hardly as clear as I could wish") and that he is not the rational, detached intellectual type that Poirot embodies. Poirot is revealed in what he does as a vain person who is very much concerned with the impeccability of his outward appearance and who loves grand gestures and expressive mimicry ("he screwed up his cherub-like face"; "shook is head energetically"; "he made an extravagant gesture"; "shook his forefinger so fiercely"). He demonstrates his mental capacities in what he says, the strict logic of his intellect, which works with meticulous attention to detail and on the basis of exact observation. There is a kind of

incongruity between the outward appearance of the "cherub-like face" and the inner quality of a relentless persecutor of criminals.

2. Several methods are employed to show the different aspects of Poirot's complex character. As was said in the above answer his actions reflect his vanity and his predilection for self-portrayal. In the analysis of the process of reconstructing a crime he demonstrates the precise working of his mind. Finally, in his language, he shows the same straightforward logic to be found in his thinking. Everything is reduced to single steps in small syntactical units. Questions, exclamations, and statements are used to stand for doubts, surprise findings, and solutions, respectively. The French expletive insertions are allusions to his Belgian nationality, but they never contain anything of importance. The different methods of characterisation combine well to create the picture of a man who does not outwardly manifest his inner qualities and who, involuntarily, seems initially to evoke mirth rather than respect. The reader is not told what to think of Poirot, but asked to make up his own mind on the basis of the information he is provided with.

4. Class Enemy

1. In this text a teacher is confronted with three of his pupils, Iron, Snatch, and Sky-Light, of whom Iron takes on the role of spokesman. The teacher is characterised as being a slightly arrogant person who has not succeeded in implanting his ideals regarding education, life and manners in his pupils and who is not really willing to make any further attempts at doing so. As far as he is concerned the pupils are the epitome of insolence, ignorance, and filth, with an utter incapacity to appreciate the benefits of education. The pupils do not even contradict their teacher's opinion, explaining that their destructive behaviour is the result of their social status; as they possess nothing, why should they show any respect for anything. They feel they are at the mercy of the teacher and others who, like him, represent the socially and economically dominating class. There is no common ground and the only way for them to be accepted would imply the denial of their social background, the subordination to other people's standards and, consequently, the possible loss of identity.

2. The incompatibility of standards of the two groups confronting each other in this scene is made obvious by the kinds of language used. The teacher chooses his words in accordance with his profession and his attendant feeling of superiority, in other words, he speaks more or less

standard English. The pupils use a strikingly different kind of language which is grammatically incorrect (when standard English is taken as the norm), full of slang and vulgar expressions and marked by a conspicuous sociolect (often known as a social dialect, referring to a language spoken by members of a particular social class or occupational group) which shows clearly that they belong to a class regarded as lower partly because of the way its members speak. The class barrier is also a linguistic barrier. Especially in the United Kingdom, where social and occupational recognition seem inevitably connected with having the proper command of standard English (there is, for example, a Society for the Preservation of the Queen's English), speakers of other sociolects are discriminated against and remain socially second-rate, if not worse. In conclusion, this particular method of characterisation quite effectively underlines the subject of the scene.

5. Lord of the Flies

1. This text extract presents the classical conflict between a protagonist (Ralph) and his antagonist (Jack), fighting for supremacy. Jack, who apparently called this meeting to decide finally on the leadership of the hunters, displays traits of threat and aggression ("he glowered up under his eyebrows"; "he said in tones of deep meaning, and menace") as well as signs of extreme helplessness, as is reflected in the loss of his voice and the avoidance of meeting the others' eyes at the culminating point of the conflict. The tension of the decisive moment and Jack's realisation that he is losing the showdown make him tremble and weep ("the hands that held the conch shook"; "paying no heed to the steady fall of his tears"). He experiences the defeat in his struggle for power as an injustice, a humiliation, and an attack on his human dignity to which he responds with infuriation and a rejection of the hunters' decision. He is by no means prepared to subordinate himself to Ralph's leadership. Ralph, however, stays in the background, although the hunters seem to be under his influence or spell; they appear as the intimidated and silent majority.

2. Various methods of characterisation are to be found in this extract. Jack characterises himself through his addresses to the hunters, although a great deal of his characterisation results from the narrator's description and evaluation. Jack's self-characterisation reveals his futile attempt at convincing the hunters, his unwillingness to accept Ralph as the leader, and his subsequent breakaway into escapism. The information given by

the narrator expounds Jack's psychic condition at this moment of extreme tension, his infuriation, his helplessness and obvious physical suffering ("painful rush"; "he licked his lips"), his feeling of humiliation, and his loss of self-control ("his voice tailed off"; "then cried out, high-pitched, enraged").

Ralph is characterised by Jack's comments as someone devoid of any merits and thus not qualified to deserve the boys' confidence; secondly, by the narrator as a somewhat alert person ("and until he dived into the forest Ralph watched him"); finally Ralph characterises himself rather succinctly ("All this talk!" shouted Ralph. "Talk, talk! Who wanted it? Who called the meeting?"), sounding quite determined. The hunters are only characterised by the narrator, who depicts them as images of uniformity, full of sheepish shame and embarrassment regarding their conduct and apparently feeling highly uncomfortable in their situation ("most of the boys were looking down now, at the grass or their feet").

The variety of the methods of characterisation employed in this text relies on the varied modes of presentation such as direct speech and authorial evaluation (elements of telling and showing). This combination of methods of characterisation, however, proves its effectiveness in that the reader acquires a deeper insight into the nature of Jack's character. The conflict and the characters' motives and responses are very well presented and the reader gets involved in the gripping tenseness of the antagonism of the situation.

6. Zigger Zagger

1. The main person characterised in this text extract is Harry Philton. He is portrayed, patronisingly, by those in official capacities who have to deal with him – the policeman, dentist, headmaster, caretaker, teacher. These figures of authority also manage to betray aspects of their own characters while focusing attention on Harry. They are seen as not being in touch with the realities surrounding them ("Don't listen to those fellers. ... They don't know.").

Harry comes from a socially less salubrious part of town where those lower down the social class ladder are forced to congregate, "them in the blocks". The automatic responses of the policeman, etc. to a character appraisal of Harry are generalising and condemnatory ("he's just like the rest of them"). He is careless of his health ("a mouth full of gums"); intellectually inadequate ("Stupid"); lacks any respect for material possessions ("he chews the ends off pencils"; "He drills holes in the protractors"), or gratitude for his lot ("It's the free milk. I wouldn't give them free milk."); degenerate ("It's only the likes of me knows what they do with the dirty straws."); dishonest, almost criminal ("I think he pinches the rubbers."). Nevertheless, in contradiction to these exceedingly disapproving stances, there is, according to the newsagent, a good side to Harry. He demonstrates an enviable diligence and sense of work ethics in his part-time job as paperboy, an attitude that would presumably be repudiated by the others as not being part of the lower class make-up.

2. The narrator has been eliminated from this text, as is generally the case in drama. Instead, Harry Philton is characterised in this passage by those in authority he has to confront. Their views on Harry are defamatory. Taken collectively these views are meant to represent a general attitude to people like Harry. The denigrating statements are repeated by several of the speakers ("He's just like the rest of them"). Ignorance is another of the conclusions reached at collectively ("I would say that if he has to hold two ideas in his head at the same time, it's a severe case of overcrowding."). The reader is given a seeming variety of attitudes, but through the repetition of statements voiced, there emerges a close and intended affinity between the individuals. Significantly, this group all leave the stage together. However, there is one adult character who counters these standpoints. The newsagent expresses admiration for Harry and his attitude to work, while he is extremely critical of the "dentists, teachers, social workers". In narrative terms, this inclusion of the newsagent is a corrective measure to balance out the deprecatory remarks of the other adult figures. The reader is still left to decide for himself, although the intervention of the newsagent does resemble authorial comment. Nevertheless, the reader is at no stage told explicitly what to think. After all, what justification is there for giving greater credibility to what the newsagent has to say than to the collective judgment of more respected (?) members of society?

7. A Christmas Carol

1. Scrooge is portrayed as a person who views his fellow men and his surroundings with a kind of indifference and standoffishness; not even the most extreme weather conditions leave any impression on this resolute but unsociable person. He appears as a lonely, reclusive person, full of indifference to others' needs and interests, surrounded by an aura

of inaccessability. Scrooge regards some of the most natural human habits as rather annoying, i.e. conversing with other people on the street, having friends, giving advice and answering inquiries, responding to requests and entreaties from the needy. The people around Scrooge, and even the animals, sense the aloof nature of his personality, and his endeavour to keep away from the everyday social bustle. It is, however, precisely this hermit-like inner seclusion and his reluctance to show natural human feelings which represents Scrooge's way of life and the main source of his personal satisfaction.

2. Scrooge is entirely characterised by authorial description and comment, a method which results particularly from the omniscient point of view and the telling mode of presentation employed in this extract. The narrator relates observations, e.g. about the interrelationship between Scrooge and the passers-by in the street, which throw a light upon Scrooge's attitude towards his fellow men; moreover, he also conveys his personal assessment of Scrooge's disposition (e.g. in comparing the extremity of his character to the extreme weather conditions), and portrays Scrooge's likes and dislikes. The narrator also dwells on the protagonist's motives for conducting his life the way he does, so completely deviant from the so-called standard behaviour of other human beings. This authorial method of presentation, although devoid of any multiplicity of perspectives, proves effective in that the reader is provided with a comprehensive view of Scrooge's character and mentality, without any degree of sympathy on the part of the narrator.

8. So You Think You Could Sell?

1. This newspaper advertisement provides the reader with characterisations of both the employing company, the *Observer*, and the kind of applicant wanted to fill the vacancy offered. In accordance with the exceptionally high standards of the *Observer*, the trainee should be endowed with a number of character traits in order to qualify for this position as professional salesperson. The qualifications regarded as indispensable include a high level of intelligence, rhetorical ability, negotiating capacity, stress resistance, commitment to the job, and the ability to achieve certain sales targets. Meanwhile the company is characterised as being a good employer by promising attractive benefits in return, such as a review of payment, and fringe benefits according to the trainee's achievement and success, and good prospects of promotion.

2. In this text the advertiser characterises himself to the prospective applicant throughout ("our standards are very high and only exceptional people are likely to succeed with us"; "... our young, dynamic team"; "once you are a member of our impressive team"). The principal method of characterisation employed in the text, however, lies in the description of the essential characteristics, activity, and remuneration of potential candidates, comprising an ability to cope with the employer's high standards; the trainee's formal and personal qualities; field of work (business and sales); earnings and benefits; prospects of promotion. The enumerative structure of the characteristics and situation mentioned displays a great deal of information about the company, job, and kind of applicant, thus enabling interested readers to gain a detailed impression of the type of employment on offer. Consequently, the methods of characterisation to be found in this text prove to be effective in that they serve the above-mentioned purposes of this newspaper advertisement well.

9. Saturday Afternoon

1. One hot Saturday afternoon Tom Denny, the butcher, is wakened from his midday nap in his shop by the news that Will Maxie, a successful black cotton farmer, is to be lynched following the allegation that he dared address a white woman in the street. The real motive for this dire deed, however, is the envy of the village's white population resulting from Will's economic success and his moral integrity. Will Maxie is brutally lynched in an atmosphere marked by ribaldry, sensationalism, and emotional indifference and insensitivity to the victim. Tom then returns to his shop to serve his customers as usual.

2. Tom Denny is a dirty, lazy butcher whose daily routine of selling meat has become a ritual of trite, meaningless, unvarying phrases and gestures. In his attitude towards blacks he reveals the stock white prejudices based on the idea of the natural dominance of the white race and the consequent right to punish any action by non-whites that could be interpreted as demonstrating a lack of humility. The belief in a 'master race' and a 'slave race' is rigidly maintained in correspondence to a reality in this text which shows nothing but white decadence, lethargy and torpor. Tom is in good spirits, self-satisfied after the murder because Will Maxie represented a threat to Tom's view of the world and his presence brought out the mediocrity of the whites. The return to the daily routine symbolises Tom's adherence to anachronistic views which accommodate

the possibility of an easy untroubled life without change and minus any feelings of inferiority.

The other characters are not presented in any great detail. What they do have in common is an amazing degree of emotional callousness which makes them envisage the lynching either as a welcome break from their normal daily routines (Jim, Hubert) or as an additional opportunity which can be commercially exploited (Doc Cromer). Whereas Tom is presented by the narrator through his actions and thoughts, thus providing the reader with a vivid impression of the unpleasantness of his character, the others are only described through the intermittent interventions of Tom's thoughts concerning the aspects he considers important (e.g. Hubert makes good corn whisky and buys meat regularly). The same is true of Will Maxie whom Tom sees as an immediate rival ("He made more money than Tom and Jim made in the butcher shop.") and a moral challenge ("he lived with his own wife").

The most important means of characterisation here are the setting (see next answer) and the particular use of language. Tom stubbornly repeats certain sentences in order to give weight to the offences which 'justly' result in Will's ritual death ("Will could grow good cotton. He cut out all the grass first, ... He always cut out the grass first ... He made too much money by taking out the grass..."). All this leads up to the real offence: "He was too damn good for a negro." The language shows Tom as a very simple-minded character for whom fixed categories and norms are indispensable; he is someone who needs a rigidly structured society and who is unable to cope with change. His own self-respect depends on the assumption that the blacks will always be inferior to him, that they do not have the right to challenge the superiority of the whites. The monotony of his life is mirrored in the repetitious use of certain phrases in his speech.

3. The plot requires a setting in an area where the claims of the whites remain unquestioned and unchallenged. By setting the scene in a small village (only *one* butcher shop) the effect of this spatial narrowness on the intellectual horizons of the inhabitants is underlined. The moral repulsiveness of the deed, i.e. the vicious murder of an innocent man in an almost funfair-like atmosphere, is matched by the repulsive conditions in the butcher shop, which no one seems to mind. The beginning and end of the story, which take place in these filthy surroundings, are longer than the middle section containing the lynching. What will go on is the monotony of life; what will remain is the dirt, the shallow small talk, the desire for sensations which are, however, short-lived. The unbearable heat of a summer noon and the perpetual existential struggle are the

preliminaries to a bloody deed. Yet hardly any difference is made between the killing of a human being and the chopping off of a pound of pork. The unimportance of the lynching, the total lack of any moral response or feelings of indignation or guilt are expressed in the title of the story: after all, it is just a normal 'Saturday Afternoon'.

Chapter V

Stylistic Devices

1. The Declaration of Independence

1. This text extract contains the opening paragraphs of the proclamation made by the American Continental Congress on July 2/4, 1776, which asserted the freedom and independence of the 13 Colonies from Great Britain. The document is a formal pronouncement of the right to government by choice and contract, and affirms the natural rights of man.

2. This text is a declaration of the rights and freedom of man. To emphasise these natural rights, their unquestionable merits and sacrosanct character the text has been composed in a grand and solemn style, the language formal ("endowed", "unalienable", "Prudence", "hath"), almost biblical ("all men are created equal", "Creator", "while evils are sufferable"), the punctuation modest to allow for as little interruption as possible in the flow of rhetoric. The text builds up to a number of minor climaxes in the form of accumulations of aspects of man's rights ("that all men are created equal, that they are endowed with..., that among these..."). This accumulation is paired with the parallelism of syntactical structures, i.e. clauses in which these rights are presented as facts, rather than simply as claims. The accumulative (and alliterative) layout of "Life, Liberty, and the pursuit of Happiness" also recreates a gravity in keeping with the seriousness of the subject. The repetitious use of syntactical units is carried on into the second paragraph ("That to secure these rights... that whenever any Form of Government") to underline the legitimacy of the rights proclaimed. Furthermore, the fact that the key positive nouns in the text (Life, Liberty, Happiness, Government, Right of the People, Safety, Prudence) are capitalised highlights the universal dimension attributed to the message.

This document is an expression of the demand for democracy, and political and natural freedom, a subject not to be treated lightheartedly. This grave subject, fundamental to the entire human race, merits the rhetorical solemnity exuded by the text. The formal eloquence generates an air of irrefutable legality and credibility in the declaration.

2. The Constitution of the United States of America

1. This text extract is the preamble or introductory statement attached to the Constitution of the United States of America, setting forth its purpose, i. e. laying down the political principles on which the USA is governed, in particular in terms of the rights of the individual.

2. The style and aims of this text are comparable with those of the Declaration of Independence. The text is laden with stylistic devices, the language is formal, the conclusion is climactic. Structurally, the text is straightforward. In the one sentence there is a parallelism of syntax (infinitive clauses of purpose), an accumulation of confident-sounding verbs ("form", "establish", "insure", "provide for", "promote", "secure") and of key positive concepts in capital letters ("Union", "Justice", "Tranquility", "Welfare", "Blessings of Liberty", "Posterity") leading up to the dramatic culmination of the Constitution and ultimately of the country itself, the embodiment of all the above virtues. The royal "we" stresses the significance of the people in this political process, thus adding the essential human dimension and the notion of unity and placing them in the forefront, above the abstractness of the other concepts.

And, as in text 1, the formality of linguistic register and the density of rhetorical devices do justice to the import of the document.

3. An Irish Airman foresees his Death

1. This Yeats poem treats the balanced awareness of an airman that he will soon be killed in action. He reviews his reasons for fighting and his attitude to life and death while yielding to his fate.

2. The feature that prevails in this text is that of balance, both in terms of content and composition. The Irish airman contemplates his forthcoming death and considers his attitudes to war, and to life in a balanced, unemotional fashion throughout ("foresees", "I know that I shall meet my fate", "I balanced all", "In balance"). The balanced nature of these reflections is effectively stressed in structural terms as well. This begins with the parallelism of lines 3 and 4. The antithesis contained in these two lines emphasises the stable nature of his deliberations. A similar balanced antithesis can be seen in lines 7 and 8. This structural balance can be traced through the entire text. The repetition in lines 5 and 6 ("my country", "my countrymen") and the emphatic anaphora of "nor" in lines 9 and 10 are further examples of the consistency of the text's

compositional layout. In lines 9 and 10 the airman as speaker coolly presents a list of the motives for fighting that he dismisses, i.e. social or moral obligations, political arguments or national sentiment. His motivation is not the collective patriotism of others but, in distinct contrast, "a lonely impulse of delight" (11). However, at no stage in the text does the airman neglect the well-balanced discursive attitude to his fate. In fact, the frequency of structural balance increases, underlining the intellectual strength of the airman ("I balanced all, brought all to mind", line 13; note the emphasising repetition of "all"). The repetition of "I balanced" (13) and "In balance" (16) highlights explicitly the nature of his response to his fate. We can detect the breadth of his analysis in the contrasting references to "the years to come", "the years behind" encasing the repeated phrase "waste of breath" (anadiplosis). He would seem to be pointing resignedly to the insignificance of life, past and future. The antithetical dimension to the presentation is continued through to the final line culminating in the ultimate existential antithesis "this life, this death" (16). It would appear as if at this moment the meaninglessness of life and death becomes a paramount realisation to an airman who wishes to escape into the metaphorical clouds (lines 2 and 12), an image of the detachment with which the airman confronts his fate.

4. The Creation of the World

1. This text shows the beginning of the creation of earth by God, i.e. the creation of light, heaven, earth and seas in the first three days.

2. The syntax in this Bible extract is uncomplicated yet phrased in such a way as to create a sense of solemnity and awe in the reader. Enormous changes in the universe are initiated by simple, yet increasingly longer imperatives ("Let there be...") and their completion is announced in short, succinct statements ("and there was..."; "and so it was") and a subsequent naming ("He called..."; "and God called..."). This name-giving is preceded on three occasions (first and third day) by an evaluation, arranged in a parallel fashion and repetitiously ("God saw that the light was good"; "God saw that it was good" – twice). The final step of each change is reached by the repetition of the almost identical sentences "Evening came, and morning came, the first day/a second/third day." In the remainder of the text there is a predomination of parallelism and accumulation intended to stress the degree of disorder before the beginning of creation (first day); to specify the imperatives on the third day, and to state the result ("so it was..."). In this way, by the use of wieldy,

identifiable, and comprehensible stylistic devices an effective contrast is created between the matter-of-fact style and the significance and enormity of events. God's power is stressed, and even the creation of earth is nothing to waste too many words on. The reader is left to wonder in admiration and reverence.

5. Anthem for Doomed Youth

1. This sonnet is a (First World War) war poem dealing with the tragic loss of a generation of young people in a conflict of barbaric dimensions. Reference is made to both the agony and death on the battlefield and the private helpless bereavement at home.

2. A sonnet poem is a text with a very formal composition, making it easier for the reader to identify the separate units, in this case, an eight-line first section (octet) and a six-line second section (sestet). This division is accentuated by the rhetorical questions in lines 1 and 9 and emphasised (content-wise) by the focus on the battlefield in the first section and on home in the second.

Basically, the poem is about wartime slaughter and bereavement. The tragic loss of a generation of young men ("Doomed Youth") is experienced as being even more bitter because of the intolerably humiliating 'farewell' arranged for them. The degradation of their deaths is alluded to as early as line 1 through the simile "those who die as cattle". These young soldiers, nothing more than cannon fodder, die lonely ignominious deaths (this fact is underlined by the anaphora – "only" – in lines 2 and 3). Their funeral is in fact nothing more than personified military conflict. Their funereal march comprises the sounds of battle ("rifles' rapid rattle"; "shrill demented choirs of wailing shells"). The onomatopoeic sounds of rifle fire are the personified prayers 'read out' with little feeling ("hasty orisons") at their battlefield grave. The absence of any genuine ceremony is further emphasised by the repetition of "no" and "nor" in the second half of the octet (lines 5 and 6), no hypocritical sermons about righteousness and patriotism, no ceremonial ritual. The narrator does introduce, temporarily, a hint of interest and concern, in the mini-climax "save the choirs", as if some sincere symbol of sorrow has been salvaged; but this hope is swiftly dashed in the next line as the focus returns to the incessantly raging battle, and dying is only ever accompanied by "the shrill demented choirs of wailing shells".

The second section ("from sad shires") lacks the noise of battle. Instead it is marked by the physical signs of grief ("pallor"), replacing more tangible funeral rituals ("pall") – tears in the eyes of boys, "the pallor of girls' brows", the memories of the "doomed youth". Those left at home are just as powerless to redirect their fate as are the young soldiers on the battlefield. The final line of the poem becomes a metaphor for the continuing grief and mourning that remains unchanged even as time passes "each slow dusk".

To what extent war poetry can be classified in terms of good and bad poetry is a question that must remain unanswered at this stage. The interaction of topic, language, structure, effect and intention would have to be considered. However, what Owen does succeed in communicating is the hypocrisy (note the title and in particular the use of the word "anthem", normally used in a more honourable context), the agony ("shrill demented", "wailing"), and the loss and mourning involved in the massacre of young soldiers in war.

6. Myth & Fact

1. This text – an advertisement in the weekly political journal, the *New Statesman* – is a publicity text in support of the Greater London Council, the municipal council responsible for the running of London and now abolished at the behest of a Conservative Government hostile to its method of running a city, and to its political beliefs and priorities. The text illustrates the controversy surrounding the cost and effectiveness of the GLC.

2. This text is structured according to antithetical views. However, the intention is to influence the reader to turn in favour of the objective *facts* and reject the bland inaccuracy of the *myths*. Three myths in the left-hand column are matched by three facts in the right-hand column. This seemingly well-balanced for-and-against situation – the listing and repetition of *myth* and *fact* (anaphora) – is, however, nothing more than a visual delusion. The contrasts are not as evenly balanced as would at first sight appear. Firstly, the texts on the left are much shorter than those on the right and are bland, imprecise, lacking in informative evidence. They are intended as denunciations of the financial extravagance, expensive bureaucracy, and superfluity of the GLC. These accusations are set against the claims put forward by the GLC – detailed and backed up by statistics (references to dates, percentage expenditure, staff size, wage bill) – that in fact it is relatively thrifty, minimally bureaucratic and that its abolition would leave the city's population democratically adrift. All six passages are quotes, yet the antithetical structure is presented with

weighted arguments in favour of the GLC. The visual and rhetorical climax to the discussion takes the form of a concluding slogan at the end of the text included as a final appeal for the retention of the GLC. So, while initially the text would appear balanced both structurally and in terms of content, it very soon becomes clear that we are dealing with a blatant propaganda exercise the success of which not only depends on the rhetoric of the text but also on the political climate at the time of its publication. (Fortunately for the GLC the Conservatives were suffering from a mid term-of-office depression. Nevertheless, the abolition was a virtual foregone conclusion.)

7. Little by Little

1. This text propagates the belief – based on statistical evidence – that in contrast to the past, when cancer in its various forms was virtually incurable, it is now being combated with a significant degree of success.

2. This propagatory text opens with a modest ("Little by little") but determined and confident claim that "the fight against cancer is being won". This pronouncement is then followed by an accumulation of antitheses based on what the medical situation was like in the past ("once", "fifteen years ago", "twenty years ago") and today. The importance of the present situation is underlined by the repetition of "today". The past situational reports on the fight against cancer, intentionally, make for depressing reading – "an almost certain killer"; "no effective treatment"; "two or three active anti-cancer drugs". The contrast is intended to be dramatic, and the degree of progress is highlighted by the scientific quoting of figures (90%, 50%, between 30 and 40) as opposed to the verbalising of figures (fifteen, twenty, two or three) in the references to the past. The aim of this presentation is to point out the magnitude of the scientific advances being made in the field of cancer research. However, while the text emits a feeling of conviction and accomplishment, it does conceal part of the harsh reality. The antithetical presentation is relative; the lack of progress in the past permits a greater glorification of the progress to date. Seen in the broader, more testing context of the illness itself the progress remains inconsiderable. A conclusion of this kind is hinted at, significantly but paradoxically, at the very beginning of the text when the pace of success is charted as progressing "Little by little". Were it placed at the end of the text, this summary would have been something of an anti-climax following the accumulative build-up of successes prior to it.

8. Julius Caesar

1. This is the first part of Antony's speech (Forum speech) in which he tries to convince the people that Brutus' motives for killing Caesar were not honourable, but were to satisfy his own ambitions, although he was aware that Caesar was innocent.

2. The key-words in this speech are the adjectives "ambitious" and "honourable", which are repeatedly used in changing contexts with different meanings. In the first part of his speech Antony speaks in syntactically straightforward language, resorting mostly to antithetical or contrasting patterns ("to bury, not to praise" – l. 76; "The evil – The good" ll. 77/8). These linguistic antitheses lead to the implicit character contrast between Caesar's alleged ambition (note the hypothetical if-clause, l. 81) and Brutus' honourableness. In the second part this contrast is openly repeated three times, almost chorus-like (note: "But" – ll. 88, 103; "Yet" – ll. 95, 100), though the references to Caesar's life and activities, all public events, would seem to clearly contradict the validity of Brutus' assertion. It becomes clear that the repetition serves the purpose of ironic reversal, i.e. expressing the opposite of what is meant. Through the repeated use of rhetorical questions the people are made the judges on this matter. As Antony provides the basis for the verdict that Caesar is not ambitious through the choice of examples from Caesar's life, the result (that he is not ambitious) is predictable. The last two lines return stylistically to the beginning in the use of a simple contrast ("not to disprove.../But" – ll. 102/3). On the whole, these stylistic devices, antithesis/contrast, repetition/parallelism, rhetorical question, facilitate an understanding of the message, and appeal to the level of intelligence of the people. The rhetorical questions provoke emotional involvement and are flattering as they grant the people (addressees) the (apparent) right to make up their own minds. The examples involving Caesar are well chosen because the people were mostly present, i.e. witnesses and therefore reliable judges. The suggestive nature of the text is probably only to be unravelled on the basis of a more intense intellectual analysis, which is beyond the people's horizons. Let it be remembered, however, that this speech is the answer to another speech earlier in the play; and the evidence put forward by Antony in Caesar's defence is only partially correct, as the reader knows, and as the people should have realised.

9. Another Brick in the Wall

1. This text extract is a plea for a removal of the dominance of teachers and the style and attitude of teaching in a system which leaves its schoolchildren anonymous and which is itself impersonal and inflexible.

2. This song extract is dominated by the repetitious use of a few stylistic devices intended to hammer home its message, rhythmically and forcefully. This technique covers the emphatic syntactical parallelisms of lines 1 and 2, 4 and 5, 6 and 7. The plea is virtually a frustrated demand for release from "education", "thought control", "dark sarcasm". The repetition of "no" in each of the first three lines backs up the determination of the call. Meanwhile the anaphoric phrase "All in all" and the syntactically parallel phrase that follows in lines 6 and 7 lead up, in an atmosphere verging on resignation, to the symbolic notion of the "brick in the wall", a construct that stands in their way, an image that represents a feeling of imprisonment, that also represents the system in which the speakers are caught up in. The teacher is a representative of this rigid social structure which determines the guiding (or misguided?) principles of authority. Unfortunately, the system lacks any transparency and hinders any widening of one's horizon.

The constant repetition in the text is typical of this text form and appropriate to the rhythmic demands of the music medium. The regular recurrence of phrases is also in keeping with the frustrated and bitter protestations of the speakers.

10. Miscellaneous

1. This text selection serves the purpose of exemplifying different stylistic devices (metaphor, pun, example, anticlimax). Due to the brevity of the texts it is of course neither useful nor possible to summarise the individual examples. Rather students should be given the opportunity to examine the basis on which different stylistic devices work and have an effect on the text.

2. The first text is an example of a metaphor. An implied comparison is made between two concepts which are normally not associated with each other. An analogy is created between an old man and a tattered coat (i.e. a worthless coat without any further use), acting as a comment on the worth or use of an aged man. Furthermore, an allusion is made to the image of a scarecrow ("A tattered coat upon a stick"), which also has the connotation of being out of use and of no value whatsoever.

The following four texts are examples of puns. Puns are humorous plays on words which are either identical or similar in sound but different in meaning. This play on words can work on different text levels: on the lexical or the syntactical level.

The "Motto" is an example of a pun which works on the syntactical level. The word "fast" has two different meanings *(quickly; go on a diet)*, reinforced by the different syntactical structures of the two sentences. In the first instruction "fast" is used as an adverb qualifying the verb "eat", thus forming a unit of verb and adverb. The next order reveals a completely different syntactical structure. By using a colon after "eat" two distinct orders are created in this sentence. In order to understand and appreciate this pun fully the right intonation is also vital. There has to be a pause after "eat" in the second set of instructions.

All the following examples of puns work on the lexical level. The pun in the third text makes use of two different meanings of the word "please": first it is used as a transitive verb, meaning *wish* or *choose*; in the second part of the sentence "please" is an intransitive verb, meaning *give satisfaction to.*

The next pun also works on the lexical level, making use of two words pronounced in the same way but different in both meaning and spelling: "bier" and "beer". Firstly, the wooden stand for a coffin is referred to; the humorous effect, however, is achieved by the allusion to the dead man's vice. Alcohol was presumably the cause of his death. It would appear to be appropriate for his friends to pay their last respects to him by carrying the beer!

The pun in the extract from **Romeo and Juliet** makes use of the different meanings of "grave". The word can be used as a noun, meaning *you shall find me a man in his grave*, or as an adjective in the sense of *earnest* or *solemn.*

The humorous effect of the short conversation between Punch and Judy is based on the intentional ambiguity of the word "free". Judy uses the expression "free speech" on purpose, knowing full well that Punch will understand "free" as meaning *liberal* or *uncensored.* She, however, means a telephone call *free of charge.*

The dictionary definition of "irony" is used to illustrate the stylistic device of the example. First, two different meanings of the word are explained, then an example is given for the application of the word. The theoretical definition is thus illustrated by an example.

The last text in this group is an example of anticlimax. In listing what was destroyed by the bomb the narrator moves from comparatively small objects (cinema, houses) to larger and more important ones (Cathedral), thus fuelling the expectation of something grand or spectacular to follow. Instead, there is a sudden transition from an idea of significance to something extremely trivial by comparison (dustbin), thus causing the humorous effect.

11. In Memoriam

1. This short text (obituary) is the public reminder (1969–1983) of the death of a member of the Hayes family. It also contains the family's commiserations.

2. Although the text deals with a person's death the references to death are indirect, euphemistic (In Memoriam = in memory of; passed away), as if the unpleasantness of dying and death were to be glossed over, hidden. Instead, the text tries to create the atmosphere of pathos, of grief and sorrow, especially through a particular use of language. The text is published in a newspaper, yet the situation recreated is ceremonious, religious, poetic, through the use of Latin ("In Memoriam"), of archaic syntax and forms ("be"; "thy"), parallelism ("in him... for him..."). The aim of these stylistic devices is to reflect the sincerity of the family's loss, and to focus attention on the positive Christian prospect of life after death. At the same time the message is meant to exude a feeling of humility and self-denial. As already pointed out the text has a double function: a) to inform (event, date, people involved); b) to publicly express private grief. The former is successful in its concise factuality, whereas the latter is almost excessive in its expression of loss.

12. The Thought-Fox

1. The poem takes the writing of poetry as its theme. It deals with the agonies and inspirations of writing poetry. The creation of a poetic text is the subject of the same poetic text. The poet uses the fox and his movements throughout as his image.

2. The poem opens with the dramatically coined metaphor of the 'thought-fox', a verbal creation that brings together the abstract notion of inspiration and the physical presence of the poetic image of the fox, a predator that hunts alone, is hunted, keeps to a nocturnal environment. The narrator traces the movements of the animal through the forest and in so doing conveys the hesitant, cautious, and determined movements of

his own mind. The animal is the physical and poetical embodiment of the creative inspiration sought after by the poet.

The poem's opening line is marked by the alliterative *m*, which forcefully stresses the comparative situation of scene/"midnight moment" and mind/"imagine". Both the idea of midnight's darkness and the forest are devices connotative of the state of mind of the artist at the outset of the creative process. The notion of (winter) darkness is repeated in line 7 (see alliterative "deeper within darkness") and is intended as an indication of the dearth of inspirational ideas. Meanwhile, the forest (1) and its associate features – snow (9, 13); trees (14); stump and hollow (15); clearings (17) – are indications of the obstacles confronting the fox, and metaphorical representations of the trials and tribulations of working towards the discovery and completion of a poetic text. We are in fact dealing here with the "forest" of the narrator-poet's mind. As time goes on and the text proceeds so the fox takes shape, becomes more familiar with the terrain, while the poet becomes more in tune with his subject and his work takes shape. As the fox probes, so the poet experiments.

At the beginning the vulpine inspiration is an indefinable phenomenon which only gradually sheds its anonymity (see anaphoric use of "something" in lines 2 and 6 for the sake of emphasis). At this point, the poet is very much on his own (repetition of "loneliness" in lines 3 and 8, epiphora). And yet, while the fox is not yet visible and while the page is still blank, the text is not static. It is "alive"; the colon at the end of line 1 creates suspense; there is movement, and this sensation is achieved by the sparing use of punctuation, of the frequent employment of run-on lines (enjambement), indicative that, while at times stuttering and slow, progress is being made all the time.

The presentation of the image of the fox is encased in a frame formed by the first five lines of the poem together with the final stanza. This structural parallelism is underlined by the additional frame of the "blank page" in line 4 and the "page is printed" in line 24. Likewise, the ticking clock (a reference to the march of time) and the window (yet another frame; also an 'eye' through which one can identify and view the development of events and thoughts) form a structural frame (3, 5; 23) linking the poet's situation to the predatory explorations of the fox.

The fox makes his first explicit appearance in line 10, when we see the cautious animal diffidently inspecting each twig and leaf (the wariness of the inspection, and the care taken, is emphasised by the repetitious use of "now" in lines 11 and 12). In fact, only selected features of the fox are focused on; however, this metonymous presentation of the animal's vigilant nostrils and particularly of the metaphorical eyes of the fox concentrates attention on the probing organs of the animal and, figuratively, of the poet's experimental searching. The increasing confidence of both the fox (see the alliterative "a body that is bold", line 16, and the repetition of "come" and "coming", lines 16 and 20) and the poet reach a climax as the fox enters the clearings – space for freedom of movement (fox) and thought (poet) – minus any obstacles, as the metonymous "eye" directs its attention „Brilliantly, concentratedly" (19) on the subject in question, a climax that culminates in the use of the word "Till" (21). However, from this point onwards there is a distinct element of distaste and anti-climax in the text. The unpleasantness of and disgust for the fox ("sudden sharp hot stink") are highlighted, as if, in figurative terms, the completion of the poem leaves behind a feeling of emptiness and rejection rather than exhilaration in the artist. The fox significantly disappears into "the dark hole of the head". The process of creation and discovery would seem to be more fascinating and tantalising than the satisfaction of presenting the finished product.

As to the effectiveness of the stylistic devices used in this text one has to limit one's comments on their appropriateness to personal judgments. It would appear, however, that Hughes has been able to present realistically and credibly an image that requires little textual exploitation to represent the less tangible notion of inspiration and creativity.

13. In Church

1. This poem is devoted to the speaker's struggle to find comfort and meaning in religion. The church would seem to offer him nothing but a chilly and lifeless atmosphere and an impression of desertion and insignificance; even the cross offers the speaker little consolation or meaning in life and religion.

2. At the beginning of this poem the speaker meditates on the meaning of religion from his personal experience, reflecting on the solemn subject matter very rationally ("Often I try/To analyse...", ll. 1/2). The narrative style of this poem (note the run-on lines throughout the poem) contributes to the speaker's controlled intellectual attempt at defining his/man's faith (note the broadening of perspective in the phrase "*our* prayers have failed/To animate", ll. 10/11). The speaker's deliberations are paralleled structurally in his observations of the inside of the church ("I have stopped to listen", l. 4). He observes how the tiny number of the faithful actually disturb the lifeless silent harmony of the church ("... the air *recomposing* itself", l. 6). Man's religious quest and the lack of answers

are made evident by the fact that darkness and silence dominate. In other words, there is a lack of enlightenment and response. In this context the light vs. dark contrast gains rhetorical significance; the approaching night ("Shadows advance/... to take possession", ll. 11/12) signifies relief for the church ("the uneasiness of the pews/Ceases", l. 15) from the unwelcome disruption of daytime and the confrontation with the inquisitive worshipper (note also the limited amount of time available to the worshipper in the phrase "the light held/For an hour", ll. 13/14). The church edifice is personified ("*body* that our prayers have failed/To *animate*", ll. 10/11; "hard ribs", l. 9). This personification of the church reinforces its lifelessness, thus elevating the contrast of light and darkness to the level of the dialectic of life and death; religion would seem to be inaccessible, dead to modern man. The church, the poetic representation of religion and the divine, provides no answers.

It is also worth noting the changing narrative perspective in the poem (I, my, our, a man, his) as the narrator's meditations and observations move from analysis to pressing interrogation and then to a more detached self-examination, and all with one aim in mind: to get closer to a religion and deity that would appear to be abandoning him.

Where visual perception is marred by darkness, auditory perception prevails. The image of the speaker repeatedly nailing (or even hammering) his questions on the cross (note the accumulation to be found in the sequence of "*breathing, testing* his faith/On emptiness, *nailing* his questions", ll. 18/19, but no satisfying crescendo or climax) is an obvious pointer to the Christian notions of crucifixion, death, resurrection, and redemption. The narrator prepares the reader for the climactic crucifixion leading to salvation, only to disappoint him. The cross is (figuratively) vacant, abandoned (note the metaphor of the "untenanted cross", l. 20), leaving man at a loss, offering him little hope. (Is this not the paradox of Christianity, which leaves so many questions unanswered?)

Note: The italics are the authors' own.